BELL'S CATHEDRAL SERIES:
EDITED BY GLEESON WHITE
AND EDWARD F. STRANGE

WELLS

Dawkes & Partridge, Photo.]   WELLS CATHEDRAL FROM ST. ANDREW'S SPRING.

THE CATHEDRAL CHURCH OF
WELLS

A DESCRIPTION OF ITS FABRIC
AND A BRIEF HISTORY OF THE
EPISCOPAL SEE

BY THE

REV. PERCY DEARMER, M.A.

WITH FORTY-SIX   ILLUSTRATIONS

LONDON GEORGE BELL & SONS 1898

W. H. WHITE AND CO. LTD.
RIVERSIDE PRESS EDINBURGH.

GENERAL PREFACE

THIS series of monographs has been planned to supply visitors to the great English Cathedrals with accurate and well illustrated guide-books at a popular price. The aim of each writer has been to produce a work compiled with sufficient knowledge and scholarship to be of value to the student of Archæology and History, and yet not too technical in language for the use of an ordinary visitor or tourist.

To specify all the authorities which have been made use of in each case would be difficult and tedious in this place. But amongst the general sources of information which have been almost invariably found useful are :—(1) the great county histories, the value of which, especially in questions of genealogy and local records, is generally recognised; (2) the numerous papers by experts which appear from time to time in the Transactions of the Antiquarian and Archæological Societies; (3) the important documents made accessible in the series issued by the Master of the Rolls; (4) the well-known works of Britton and Willis on the English Cathedrals; and (5) the very excellent series of Handbooks to the Cathedrals originated by the late Mr John Murray; to which the reader may in most cases be referred for fuller detail, especially in reference to the histories of the respective sees.

GLEESON WHITE,

E. F. STRANGE,

Editors of the Series.

AUTHOR'S PREFACE

THE writer about cathedrals nowadays is one who, reaping where he has not sown, and gathering where he has not strawed, is indebted for most that he says to the patient labours of other and wiser men. Nowhere does one feel this more than at Wells. The admirable Somerset Archæological Society has gone on accumulating information about the cathedral for more years than the present writer has lived. Professor Freeman produced twenty-eight years ago, in his "History of the Cathedral Church of Wells," a little book which has since been a model for all works of the kind, and of which one can still say that no one can understand all that is contained in the word "cathedral" unless he has read it. Yet since that book was written much fresh material has been discovered, and the theories then held as to the building of the cathedral have been in great measure disproved. To Canon C. M. Church, in his "Chapters in the Early History of Wells," and his papers read before the Somerset Society, we are indebted for most valuable statements of the new historical discoveries, and to his untiring kindness I am myself beholden to a greater extent than I can express.

Wells so abounds in interesting detail, that the exigencies of space have made it necessary to curtail the last chapter, which contains the history of the diocese ; a good deal of interesting matter has thus been cut from my original MS. of this chapter, and many bishops have been dismissed more summarily than they deserve. The need of dealing properly with the cathedral itself must be my apology for the baldness of this last chapter as it now stands. Those who desire a further acquaintance with the history of the diocese cannot do better than consult Mr Hunt's "Bath and Wells," in the excellent Diocesan Histories series of the Society for the Promotion of Christian Knowledge.

To many other writers on the Cathedral Church of Wells, acknowledgments and references will be found scattered throughout the present volume. I must also express my thanks to Mr Philips, and Messrs Dawkes & Partridge of Wells, for permission to reproduce their photographs, and to Mr W. Heywood and Mr H. P. Clifford for their drawings.

P. D.

CONTENTS

LIST OF ILLUSTRATIONS

WELLS CATHEDRAL

CHAPTER I

HISTORY OF THE CHURCH

"THE Gothic Cathedral," wrote Froude, an author who held no brief for the Gothic period, "is perhaps, on the whole, the most magnificent creation which the mind of man has as yet thrown out." The Cathedral Church of Wells, wrote Froude's predecessor in the same historical chair, is "the best example to be found in the whole world of a secular church, with its subordinate buildings." "There is no other place," Professor Freeman went on to say, "where you can see so many of the ancient buildings still standing, and still put to their own use." And surely there is no place better fitted to be their home than this beautiful old city of Wells, set in the midst of the fair western country, the land of Avalon and Camelot, of Athelney and Wedmore.

This unique group of buildings does not, however, take us back earlier than the close of the Norman period. Of what existed before, we have but scant evidence. Tradition says that King Ina had, about the year 705, founded at Wells a college of secular priests, and therefore a church of some sort. And when King Eadward the Elder, taking advantage of the peace which his father Alfred had secured, fixed, in 909, the new Somersetshire see by the fountain of St. Andrew at Wells, he seems to have chosen that little city because there already existed therein a church, large enough to serve as a cathedral in those times, and tended already by a body of secular canons. Now that the ancient church of St. Andrew was raised to this new dignity, it was probably in the tenth century rebuilt in stone, with plain round-headed windows, and perhaps a small unbuttressed tower to hold the bells; for, when Giso became

3

bishop in the next century (1061-1088), he erected a whole cluster of quasi-conventual buildings, but we are not told that he found it necessary to rebuild the church, although he complained that he found it mean and its revenues small.   Indeed, the fact that Giso was buried under an arch in the wall on the north side of the high altar, as his predecessor Duduc had been buried on the south side, shows that he had not rebuilt the church.

On Giso's death, John de Villula at once swept away his buildings, and set up a bishop's house on their site.   John, however, made Bath his cathedral church, and suffered the church of Wells to fall into the decay from which it was rescued by the first "Maker of Wells," Bishop Robert of Lewes.

The active episcopate of Robert of Lewes (1136-66) was as important an era in the history of the church as in that of the chapter.   In spite of the anarchy of Stephen's reign, Robert set steadily to work ; and, while the neighbouring barons were battering each other's castles, the bishop reared the first great cathedral church of Wells.   How much of the old Saxon building he left we cannot tell ; but it was in a ruinous condition, and he may have pulled it completely down, or he may have left one part for later builders to deal with.   In 1148 his new Norman church was consecrated, a massive round-arched building, its nave perhaps as large as the present one, and its choir under the tower with a small presbytery beyond.   This date may be taken as the beginning of the present cathedral ; for all the succeeding reconstructions followed the lines of Bishop Robert's church.   Yet the Norman work has disappeared almost as completely as the Saxon, and the font is the only object which can be claimed as undoubtedly Romanesque.   Of distinctly Norman mouldings there are none in the church, and only a few fragments in other places. Seldom has one of those strong Norman buildings so utterly vanished from sight.   But many stones dressed in the Norman fashion can still be traced by the expert in the eastern part of the church (p. 74), having been no doubt used up again by the later workmen ; and there may be masses of undisturbed masonry hidden in the walls.

Bishop Robert, as we know from one of his charters, did something also for the order of his church.   Mammon had gradually encroached upon the sacred precincts, and the markets had come to be held in the "vestibule," and in the church itself; the busy hum of the buyers and sellers marred the quiet of God's house, and disturbed the people at their devotions. Strong measures were necessary, and the bishop ordered the market to be held at some distance from the church, while at the same time, as an act of grace, he remitted the tolls that were due to him as lord of the manor. Thus did he lay the foundation of the liberties of Wells city while securing the sanctity of Wells Cathedral.

According to Bishop Godwin (1616), and the anonymous fifteenth century MSS., called in Wharton's *Anglia Sacra* the "Canon of Wells," there was a blank in the history of the church between Bishop Robert, who consecrated the Norman building in 1148, and Bishop Jocelin, whose episcopate lasted from 1206 to 1242. Godwin, who exaggerated a passage from the "Canon of Wells" (which that writer had produced by exaggerating a single sentence of a preamble of Jocelin, p. 7), declared that Jocelin found the church "as ready to fall," and "pulled down the greatest part of it, to witte, the west ende, and built it anew from the very foundation." This became the accepted view. But the documents recently brought to light through the labours of those who unearthed and deciphered the MSS. in possession of the chapter, have proved that the energetic Bishop Reginald, so far from letting the church go into ruin during his episcopate (1174-1191), did in reality rebuild it himself. Much travelled, conversant with all kinds of churches and cities in an age of great building operations, he was not the sort of man to neglect his cathedral. And, as a matter of fact, he is proved to have begun the present church by a charter recently found, which is of a date prior to 1180, and therefore belongs to the early years of his episcopate. In this important document, recognising his duty to provide "that the honour due to God should not be tarnished by the squalor of His house," he arranges in full chapter for a munificent grant in support of the fabric, until the work be finished.* Another charter of Reginald's time, which conveys a private gift to the church, alludes to "the admirable structure of the rising church," thus testifying to the successful progress of the bishop's plan during his own lifetime. The part which he built, there can be

* *Somerset Proceedings*, 1888, ii. 5.

little doubt, included the three western bays of the choir (which then formed the presbytery), the transepts, north porch, and the eastern bays of the nave. That is to say, on entering the church one is looking upon Reginald's work, and not Jocelin's ; for, although the rest of the nave was completed by Jocelin, it was done in accordance with Reginald's original plan.

It is of great importance to remember this fact, since until recently the nave, with the other parts just mentioned, was attributed by Professor Willis, Professor Freeman, and most authorities to Jocelin. Willis, indeed, bowed to what was then thought to be documentary evidence against his own judgment ; for he declared the work to be of a style much earlier than that of Jocelin's time (p. 73). Now we know almost to a certainty that the bulk of the cathedral belongs neither to the late Norman period of Robert, nor to the Early English of Jocelin, but to the period just between the two, that of Reginald de Bohun.

During the episcopate of Reginald's immediate successor Savaric (1192-1205), something further may have been done to the nave. But there was small opportunity for church building during this bishop's wandering and litigious life ; and all we know for certain is that, owing no doubt to the civil war, the intolerable exactions of papal legates, and the quarrel with Glastonbury, the cathedral church of Wells had fallen into a state of dilapidation when Jocelin became bishop in 1206 ; and that it remained in this condition till King John was dead : for Jocelin was an exile abroad, the property of the see was confiscated, and its income paid yearly into the king's purse.

From the year 1218, when the land was again at peace, and a profitable arrangement had been come to with the monks of Glastonbury, Jocelin devoted himself to the fabric and chapter of Wells, up to the year of his death in 1242. Grants of money and of timber, which are extant, show that by 1220 the work was recommenced, and that it was in progress in 1225. By 1239 the church was sufficiently advanced to be dedicated.

Jocelin and his brother Hugh (afterwards Bishop of Lincoln) were natives of the city they loved so well. They had both lived through Reginald's episcopate—Jocelin as canon and Hugh as archdeacon of Wells. After, when they rose to high positions as judges, and became honourably rich, Hugh, who built much in Lincoln Cathedral, gave largely of his great wealth to Jocelin for Wells, and Jocelin himself spent all that he had upon the place where he had been brought up from infancy.

Thus Jocelin was in a real sense a "maker of Wells." But he was not the only maker, for he must share the honour with two other master builders—Robert, whose work is entirely gone, and Reginald, whose work remains. He did not, as Godwin led us to suppose, pull down and rebuild the whole church. But he loyally carried on the work of his predecessor, and he executed the great work which has been always rightly attributed to him, the present west front ; this he joined to Reginald's unfinished nave by building the three western bays in strict accordance with the earlier style. The front belongs to the fully-developed Early English style in which Salisbury is built, agreeing exactly with the date of the consecration of the church by Jocelin in 1239,—as was pointed out by Professor Willis, who was puzzled by the great difference in its style from that of the nave, which was then thought to belong to the same period. We know that Jocelin was a frequent visitor to Salisbury while Bishop Poore was building it ; and thus all the lines of evidence combine to support the unshaken tradition that Jocelin was the author of the west front.

A month before his death in 1242, Jocelin de Wells put forth a charter for the increased endowment of the cathedral staff ; and it was because of a few chance words in the preamble that he came to be credited with the construction of the whole. Having found the church in danger of ruin, runs the passage, by reason of its age *aedificare coepimus et ampliare—in qua adeo profecimus—quod ipsam consecravimus*. This, which need mean nothing more than extensive building operations, is the sole foundation for the tradition that Jocelin pulled down the old church and built a new one.

The condition of the church at the end of the thirteenth century is thus described by Professor Freeman * :

" By the end of the thirteenth century we may look upon the church of Wells as at last finished. It still lacked much

* *History of the Cathedral*, p. 98.

of that perfection of outline which now belongs to it, and which the next age was finally to give to it. Many among that matchless group of surrounding buildings which give Wells its chief charm, had not yet arisen. The church itself, with its unfinished towers, must have had a dwarfed and stunted look from every point. The Lady Chapel had not yet been reared, with its apse alike to contrast with the great window of the square presbytery above it, and to group in harmony with the more lofty chapter-house of its own form. The cloister was still of wood. The palace was still undefended by wall or moat. The Vicars' Close and its chain-bridge had not yet been dreamt of. Still, the church, alike in its fabric and its constitution, may be looked on as having by this time been brought to perfection. . . . The nave, recast in forms of art such as Ina and Eadward, such as Gisa and Robert, had never dreamed of, with the long range of its arcades and the soaring sweep of its newly-vaulted roof, stood, perfect from western door to rood-loft, ever ready, ever open, to welcome worshippers from city and village, from hill and combe and moor, in every corner of the land which looked to Saint Andrew's as its mother church. The choir, the stalls of the canons, the throne of the Bishop, were still confined within the narrow space of the crossing; but that narrow space itself gave them a dignity which they lost in later arrangements. For the central lantern, not yet driven to lean on ungainly props, with the rich arcades of its upper stages still open to view, still rose, in all the simple majesty of its four mighty arches, as the noblest of canopies over the choir below."

"The eastern ending of the presbytery was," Mr Freeman proceeds, "rich with the best detail of the thirteenth century, as can be learnt from the fragments built up in the chapel of the Vicars' Close, and lying about in the undercroft of the chapter-house, which are in the full Early English style of the west front. The existing choir aisle walls prove that a procession-path ran behind the high altar, with most likely a chapel beyond it."

"The thirteenth century," he concludes, "had done its great creative work, and had left to future ages only to improve and develop according to the principles which the thirteenth century had laid down. That is to say, the thirteenth century had done for the local church of Wells what it did for England, what it did for Europe, and for the world."

The choir, however, was not so cramped as Mr Freeman thought, for it included one bay of the nave, as we now know from a notice of the making of Haselshaw's tomb, which was dug at the entrance to the choir; and, indeed, the marks where the screen was fixed are still visible on the piers at this point. From the top of the screen the great rood looked down the nave, and on each side of the doorway stood an altar, that on the north dedicated to Our Lady, that on the south to St. Andrew. The aisles of the choir were also screened off from the nave, and outside their gates were two more altars—St. Saviour's on the north, and St. Edmund's on the south. Thus the nave, where men were ever coming and going, walking and talking, and in laxer times buying and selling as well, was quite shut off from the more sacred places. Yet here, too, were altars and shrines, and here came the processions on Sundays and holidays.

Within the choir the chapter said their offices, the dean and precentor facing east in their returned stalls, and the other dignitaries in their allotted places, with the junior canons, vicars, and those in minor orders below them, and the boys on the lowest forms of all. Just beyond these stalls was the bishop's throne; and east of the tower the presbytery stood open, with the tombs of the early bishops, on either side, under the arches. The rest of the space enclosed within the screen belonged more especially to the clergy; the north transept was probably used as a chapter-house, when the undercroft was yet unfinished, and its western aisle was used as the chapter library. The chamber leading to the undercroft was the vestry, and the stout walls of the octagon, when it was finished, protected the vestments and treasures of the cathedral.

It is worth while to call to mind the kind of service for which the church was built, with its aisles and chapels and screen. The usual Sunday procession started from the north door of the presbytery, preceded by two thurifers with censers, went round behind the presbytery, the priest in his cope asperging the altars on his way, then down the south choir aisle, and through the south transept into the cloister. In the cloister-cemetery, the priest, with his ministers, said the prayers for the dead, and then rejoined the procession in the cloister Lady Chapel, where the first station was made. Thence the procession returned to the great rood in the nave, and there made the second station, the bidding-prayer being given out to the people from the rood-screen, after which it re-entered the choir. But on special occasions the ritual was increased; as, for instance, at the procession of palms on Palm Sunday, or the Corpus Christi Day procession, which is thus described by Mr J. D. Chambers * : "The procession, some time before the mass, should assemble in order at the step of the Choir (*i.e.* in the Presbytery), a priest in Albe and silk Cope carrying the Corpus Christi in a tabernacle or feretory under a canopy of silk raised over him and it on four staves, borne by four clerks in Albes and Tunicles, with lighted tapers. It should go out of the Choir down the Nave, and out at the West Door of the Church, round the Church and Cloisters as on Ascension Day "— *i.e.* round the outside of the whole church, beginning with the north side and returning round the east end, and through the cloister to the west door again, and thus back into the nave. The colours of the vestments at Wells followed in the main the custom of the neighbouring diocese of Sarum, but with some local variations, such as are set down in the *Consuetudinary* which Archbishop Laud had copied from the late thirteenth-century MS. Indigo and white were used on St. John's Day and on the Dedication Festival; in Advent, indigo; at Passiontide, red, and on Palm Sunday, "except one cope of black for the part of Caiaphas" at the singing of the Passion; red, too, on Maunday Thursday, but with a banner of white. Red was also used for Easter, Pentecost, and throughout the Sundays after Trinity; while for Virgin Martyrs, red was mixed with white. This mixture of colours was probably effected by the cantors wearing different coloured copes; thus for confessors saffron (*croceus*) was mixed with green, *sicut honestius et magis proprie possunt adaptari festo*; but St. Julian and some others had all saffron, while a few, like St. Benedict, had all indigo. White is comparatively little in evidence, but it was used at Christmas, and for commemorations of the Blessed Virgin. Black was used for the commemoration of the dead.

To this vision of stately pomp, and changing colour, we must add in our mind's eye the many chapels with their woven tapestries of flowers and beasts and birds, their rich ornaments and sacred associations; the majestic rood upon the screen,

* *Divine Worship in England*, p. 195.

and the rich altars that stood before it; the almost constant succession of services that went on behind it, where the canons (each with his own book and candle) and their vicars sat, and the pyx hung over the high altar; the sound of a little bell from one of the chapels where mass was being said, the glimmer of a hanging lamp, the gleam of a silver image, the shrines here and there, with their frequent visitors; and, as years went on, the subdued light from the gorgeous painted windows (that over the high altar glowed then from east to west without obstructing organ), the frescoes on some of the walls, the green and red and gold of the later monuments; and over all the trail of incense and the sound of prayer.

After Jocelin's death the works came to a standstill, for the sufficient reason that the chapter was "overburdened with an intolerable debt," owing to the enormous expense of the litigation with Bath Abbey over Bishop Roger's election (p. 153). This, however, was the last attempt of the rival cathedral of St. Peter; and the debt, which was at its worst in 1248 (the year after Roger's death), was bravely met by a contribution of a fifth of the income of each prebend, as well as by gifts and obits; so that towards the end of William Bytton's episcopate the debt was nearly cleared, and in 1263 Bytton made over the sequestrations of vacant benefices to the fabric fund.

In 1248 an earthquake had done much damage, shaking down the *tholus* (either the vault, or the stone capping) of the central tower, as we learn from Matthew Paris (*Hist. Angl.* iii. 42). Accordingly, in 1263, preparations were made for further building; and in 1286 we hear of a chapter meeting, summoned by Dean Thomas Bytton, whereat the canons bind themselves to give one-tenth of their prebends for five years, "to the finishing of the works now a long time begun (*jam diu incepta*), and to repair what needed reparation in the old works."

The reparation here mentioned refers in all probability to the roof and piers of the transepts and eastern part of nave, damaged by the fall of the *tholus*. The famous western capitals of the transepts, with their frequent representations of the miseries of toothache, must refer to the second William Bytton, who had died in 1274, and whose tomb became famous for its dental cures (p. 125). No doubt, the offerings at the shrine of this local saint helped considerably to swell the funds for the building operations.

The works "now a long time begun" can hardly be anything else than the chapter-house undercroft, the outer walls of which may have been built some forty years before. Professor Willis, who had access to the document, decided, on architectural evidence, that the undercroft must have been already completed at this time, and his view may be safely accepted (*Arch. Inst.*, "Bristol" vol., p. 28). The passage to the undercroft would seem to be the first result of the chapter's undertaking; its ornament is of a more advanced type than that of the undercroft itself, and one of its carved heads is swollen as by the toothache, and tied in a handkerchief. There can be little or no doubt that the "finishing" of the old works included also the building of the chapter-house staircase, and, when that was finished, the raising of the chapter-house itself (the *nova structura* of the old documents) upon the undercroft. The full Decorated style of the chapter-house is separated by a considerable interval from the late Early English of the undercroft, while that of the staircase, which is geometrical Decorated of a character not very far removed from Early English, must have been built before the chapter-house itself was begun.

The self-sacrificing spirit of the chapter was supplemented by the offerings which flowed in from the growing practice of endowing altars for requiem services, as well as from the shrine of St. William Bytton ; and the building activity continued for the next fifty years till the church had been brought, in all save its western towers, to its final state of perfection. After the staircase to the chapter-house had been completed, about the year 1292, the walls of the chapter-house itself were built, probably by Bishop William de Marchia (1293-1302) who seems to have covered it in with a temporary roof.

Dean John de Godelee (1306-1333) was the last great builder of the church of Wells. The power of the bishop in his own church is already declining, as that of the chapter rises, and it is the dean now who organises the works. In 1315 the central tower was raised, and by 1321 it was being roofed in. By 1319 the chapter-house was finished ; Godelee, with William Joy, the master-mason, had probably worked out the old drawings and built the windows and vaulted roof.

Next the Lady Chapel must have been begun, for by 1326 it was finished. Somewhere about this time the parapet, which adds so much to the external beauty of the church, was also made.

But the raising of the central tower had, ere this, brought disaster. In 1321 there was a grant from the clergy of the Deanery of Taunton in aid of the roofing of the "new *campanile*"; in 1338 a convocation was summoned because the church of Wells was so *totaliter confracte et enormiter deformate* that the instant and united action of its members was required to save it (*cf.* Willis in *Som. Proc.* 1863). The adding of the Decorated portion to the tower increased the weight so much that the four great piers sank into the ground, dragging the masonry with them and causing rents to appear at the apex of the arches. The situation was most dangerous : it was met by the careful repairing of the torn masonry and the construction of those inverted arches which are so familiar a feature of the church.

Yet the work proceeded very rapidly under a great bishop, who for the time eclipsed the rising power of the deans. Ralph of Shrewsbury (1329-63) carried on the work of Dean Godelee, and in the early years of his episcopate entirely reconstructed the choir. The scheme seems to have been contemplated as early as 1325 ; for in that year each dignitary arranged to pay for his own stall in the refitting of the choir, because the old stalls had become "ruinous and misshapen." In any case, it was Ralph who added the three new bays of the presbytery which are so curiously joined to the old presbytery of Reginald, and with it form the present eastern limb of the church. He then constructed the beautiful retrochoir which connects the presbytery with the Lady Chapel. The vaulting of the choir and the construction of the great east window would appear to have been undertaken at a later period of his episcopate ; for the ceiling is of a more advanced style than the lower work, and the tracery of the window is half Perpendicular. When Bishop Ralph died, in 1363, he was buried in the place of honour in front of the high altar, as the founder of the choir which he had finished.

The finishing touches were given to the cathedral when Bishop Harewell (*ob.* 1386) gave two-thirds of the cost of the south-western or Harewell Tower, and when the executors of

Bishop Bubwith (*ob.* 1424) finished the companion tower on the north-west.

The other efforts of the fourteenth and fifteenth century builders were given to those subordinate buildings which are the peculiar glory of Wells. Even so magnificent a prelate as Beckington did nothing to the actual fabric of the Cathedral (unless his tomb be so considered), for the simple reason that there was really nothing for him to do. Ralph of Shrewsbury had, besides his work in the church, finished the palace (which Jocelin had begun and Burnell had enriched with the hall and chapel) by the moat, walls, and gate-house. He had also begun the Vicars' Close, of which the chapel was built by Bubwith, but the executors of Beckington recast it in its present form. After Beckington had employed his energies in erecting the beautiful gateways with which his name is always associated, Dean Gunthorpe (*ob.* 1498) built the deanery.

The following interesting eulogy of Bishop Beckington and his church was written in the form of a Latin dialogue by Chaundler, who was Chancellor of Wells in 1454:—

"You might more properly call it a city than a town, as you would yourself understand more clearly than day if you could behold all its intrinsic splendour and beauty. For that most lovely church which we see at a distance, dedicated to the most blessed Apostle of the Almighty God, St. Andrew, contains the episcopal chair of the worthy Bishop. Adjoining it is the vast palace, adorned with wonderful splendour, girt on all sides by flowing waters, crowned by a delectable succession of walls and turrets, in which the most worthy and learned Bishop Thomas, the first of that name, bears rule. He has indeed at his own proper pains and charges conferred such a splendour on this city, as well by strongly fortifying the church with gates and towers and walls, as by constructing on the grandest scale the palace in which he resides and the other surrounding buildings, that he deserves to be called, not the founder merely, but rather the splendour and ornament of the church."

The Reformation period left the cathedral cold and barren within, but interfered little with its fabric; the only serious piece of destruction (p. 57) being that of the magnificent Lady Chapel by the Cloister, in 1552, by Sir John Gates, "a

The South Prospect of y Wellensis ecdi Cath.
Cathedral Church of Wells. facies australis.

In
Gratiam potentissimi
D.
Ioh: Steanqwayes
Eqi Aur:

THE CATHEDRAL. (From a Seventeenth-Century Print.)

greate puritan, Episcopacie's common Enemy." In other respects it was what Freeman calls a period of systematic picking and stealing; as witness this passage from Nathaniel Chyles :—" The Great Duke of Somersett, Unkle to Edward the Sixt (whose title proved very fatall to this place and Bishopwrick) was not only contented to get most of the mannours Lands and possessions belonging to this Bishopwrick settled upon him and his posteritie, but at last even the palace itselfe also." But the palace and some of the property were recovered after Somerset's execution.

The bishop's palace suffered the ruin of Burnell's magnificent hall through the prevalent lust for gain. Sir John Harrington writes in terms of pardonable indignation :—" I speak now only of the spoil made under this Bishop [Barlow]; scarce were five years past after Bath's ruins, but as fast went the axes and hammers to work at Wells. The goodly hall covered with lead . . . was uncovered, and now this roof reaches to the sky. The Chapel of Our Lady, late repaired by Stillington, a place of reverence and antiquity, was likewise defaced, and such was their thirst after lead (I would they had drunk it scalding) that they took the dead bodies of bishops out of their leaden coffins, and cast abroad the carcases scarce thoroughly putrified."

During the Commonwealth the choir was closed, and Dr Cornelius Burges, who was appointed "Preacher" at the cathedral, bought the bishop's palace and deanery for his private property. He, of course, despoiled the palace, "pulling off not only the Lead thereoff," says Chyles,* "but taking away also the Timber, and making what money he could of them, and what remained unsold he removed to the Deanery improving that out of the Ruins of the palace, leaving only bare Walls." At the Restoration Burges was ejected, after a good deal of litigation, and Bishop Piers returned to the ruins of his palace. Burges' sermons had never been popular with the people of Wells, who annoyed him by walking up and down the cloisters "all sermon time." When the trial for his ejectment came on he published his "Case," in which he justified his buying Church lands by alleging that he had lent the State £3490, and, having a wife and ten children to provide for, he took such land, etc. as the only means of repayment. Five of

* Book ii. c. 2.

the canons' houses were also obtained from Cromwell's Commissioners by the Corporation of Wells, one or two of which were pulled down and sold for old stone.

At the Restoration, the canons were at great expense to restore the church from the ruinous condition into which it had fallen in Puritan times, and they were liberally helped in their extremity by the clergy and laity of the diocese. Says Chyles (c. 1680): "Since his Majestie's and Churche's happy and blessed Restoration, what betweene the Bishopp, the Deane, and Deane and Chapter, our Church and Quire is once more in a beautifull and comely habitt (which God continue) such as neither the Church of Rome has reason to upbraid us with a slovenly or clownish Service, nor the Puritan and Nonconformist with a gaudy or Superstitious. The good old Bishopp [W. Piers], who weather'd out that Storme, and was restored to what was his Owne, gave those silk Hangings which beautifie the Altar within the Railes." Dean Creyghton gave the glass in the west window, the organ and the brass lectern, and Dr Busby, who was treasurer of Wells as well as head-master of Westminster, gave the silver-gilt alms dish and restored the library, lengthening it by the addition of the southern part.

Chyles tells us, too, that there was morning and evening prayer in the "Vicars' Chapell in Close Hall," at six, forenoon and afternoon, in winter, and seven in summer, in addition to the cathedral services at the "canonical howers." Before his time there had been only a morning sermon on Sundays, and, in the afternoon, "the whole Cathedrall" had been in the habit of going to St. Cuthbert's, returning with the mayor and his brethren for the cathedral prayers at four; "but since his Majesty's Restoracion one likewise in the Afternoones here is preached by the said prebends *in theire turns.* Soe that here the Sermonizing people may have their Bellyfull of preaching and forbeare crying out, *They are starved for want of the Word* and calling our clergy *Dumb Doggs.*"

This time of peace did not last long, for in 1685 the whole of Somerset was up in Monmouth's rebellion. The duke's followers came to Wells, turned the cathedral into a stable, tore the lead off the roof for bullets, pulled down several of the statues, broached a barrel of beer on the high altar, and would have destroyed the altar itself, had not Lord Grey, one of their leaders, defended it with his sword.   Dr Conan Doyle's description of the scene in his novel, *Micah Clarke* (p. 292), is so vivid that it is well worth referring to.

The long and heavy peace which followed was marked by the gradual pewing up of the choir and presbytery, and the intrusion of pretentious monuments.   Then, in our own times, came the revival, bringing evil as well as good in its train.   In 1842 the restoration of the nave, transepts, and Lady Chapel was commenced at the instance of Dean Goodenough, by Mr Benjamin Ferrey.   He removed the thick layers of whitewash which had been ingeniously applied to conceal the sculpture ; and the long rows of marble tablets which had disfigured the aisles were shifted to the cloisters, whence, it may be hoped, they will one day make a further journey towards oblivion.

The restoration of the choir by Mr Salvin, which lasted from 1848 to 1854, was unfortunately of a less blameless character. It was the period of the Great Exhibition, when art reached the lowest depths to which it has sunk in the history of the world. We need not dwell upon the result ; few restorations are more marked with the complacent ignorance of that strange time.   The old pews and galleries in the choir, which had hidden the very capitals of the piers, were indeed removed, but with them the medieval stalls were destroyed and replaced by work of indescribable imbecility.   No real improvement in the choir of Wells is now possible till every trace of Dean Jenkyns' restoration is swept away ; but, alas ! what he destroyed can never be recovered.

In 1868 the report of Mr Ferrey * upon the west front was presented, and shortly afterwards the work of repair was begun under his direction.   The report showed how extensive was the decay, and how great the danger of complete ruin unless steps were taken to protect the old work ; and the work of repair was carried out with care and reverence ; though even here irrepar-able harm was done by the substitution of the modern " slate pencils " for the old blue lias shafts.   Since then, many small matters have been attended to with varying success.   The Lady Chapel has been decently furnished and the east end slightly improved.   Much still remains to be done ; but the best motto at the present day is *festina lente*, and the safest rule is to be progressive in all enrichment by removable

* *Inst. Arch.* 1870.

furniture, and conservative, very conservative, in all structural alteration. If the hand of the restorer can now be stayed, the words will still be true of Wells, which M. Huysmans used of

Dawkes & Partridge, Photo.]

SOUTH AISLE OF NAVE. (See p. 83.

another church :—*Ces siècles s'étaient reunis pour apporter aux pieds du Christ l'effort surhumain de leur art, et les dons de chacun étaient visibles encore.*

CHAPTER II

THE EXTERIOR

"In England," wrote Mr J. H. Parker, in his *Glossary*, "Wells affords the most perfect example of a cathedral with all its parts and appurtenances. It was," he continues, after an enumeration of the parts of the church, "a cathedral proper, and independent of any monastic foundation, but with a separate house for each of its officers, either in the Close or in the Liberty adjoining to it. The bishop's palace was enclosed by a separate moat and fortified, being on the south side of the cloister, from which it is separated by the moat; the houses for the dean and for the archdeacon are on the north side of the Close, with some of the canons' houses; the organist's house is at the west end, adjoining to the singing-school and the cloister; the precentor's house is at the east end, near the Lady Chapel. The vicars-choral have a close of their own adjoining to the north-east corner of the canons' close, with a bridge across through the gate-house into the north transept; they were a collegiate body, with their own chapel, library, and hall." One need only add that all these sentences can still, with one exception, be read in the present tense to show that Wells possesses a beauty and interest which gives it an unique place among cathedral foundations. There is no other cathedral city in which so many of the old ecclesiastical buildings remain, or on which the modern world has made so little impression. The church itself, in Fergusson's opinion perhaps the most beautiful, though one of the smallest in England, is but one part of a "group of buildings, which," wrote Professor Freeman, "as far as I know, has no rival, either in our own island or beyond the sea." The little city to which these buildings belong is itself worthy of them, almost a part of them, so quiet and venerable is it, so picturesque in its lovely setting of green hills.

20

Were size the main distinction of a church, Wells would sink comfortably into the second class; even in some of its best features it has many rivals, but the peculiar charm and glory of Wells lies (to quote again from Freeman's *History*) "in the union and harmonious grouping of all. The church does not stand alone; it is neither crowded by incongruous buildings, nor yet isolated from those buildings which are its natural and necessary complement. Palace, cloister, Lady Chapel, choir, chapter-house, all join to form one indivisible whole. The series goes on uninterruptedly along that unique bridge, which, by a marvel of ingenuity, connects the church itself with the most perfect of buildings of its own class, the matchless vicars' close. Scattered around we see here and there an ancient house, its gable, its windows, or its turret, falling in with the style and group of greater buildings, and bearing its part in producing the general harmony of all." Thus, in the first place, the group of buildings must be looked at as a whole from the north, from the east, from the south-east; then the superb, unrivalled picture from the rising ground on the Shepton Mallet road,* outside the city, must be seen, and, when this little journey has been made, the most hurried visitor must find time at least to peep into the vicars' close, and walk round the moat of the palace. After some such general impression has been gained, the study of the exterior of the church will naturally begin with that part which is a peculiar distinction of Wells Cathedral— the west front.

The **West Front** of Wells has been universally admired. Long ago, old Fuller wrote—"The west front of Wells is a masterpiece of art indeed, made of imagery in just proportion, so that we may call them *vera et spirantia signa*. England affordeth not the like." This verdict is but repeated by modern writers; the front is "quite unrivalled," says Fergusson, and comparable only to Rheims and Chartres. Mr Hughes, in Traill's *Social England*, goes farther and says† that "nothing fit to rank with it was then being done in Northern Europe—for the monumental porches of France,

---

* The road should be followed for about a quarter of a mile out of the town; at this point a path leads over a stile and through a coppice to the best point of view.

† Vol. i. 421.

formerly supposed to be contemporary, are now recognised as of a later date."

But there has been a discordant note in the general chorus of praise. Professor Freeman, whose admiration for nearly everything in Wells was so intense, could find little to praise in the west front of the cathedral.* "It is doubtless," he wrote, "the finest display of sculpture in England; but it is thoroughly bad as a piece of architecture. I am always glad when I get round the corner, and can rest my eye on the massive and simple majesty of the nave and transepts. The west front is bad because it is a sham— because it is not the real ending of the nave and aisles, but a mere mask, devised, in order to gain greater room for the display of statues. . . . . The front is not the natural finish of the nave and aisles; it is a blank wall built up in a shape which is not the shape which their endings would naturally assume. It is therefore a sham; it is a sin against the first law of architectural design, the law that enrichment should be sought in ornamenting the construction . . . not in building up anything simply for the sake of effect." He then proceeds to criticise the way in which the windows and doorways "are stowed away as they best may

WEST FRONT. BISHOP AETHELHELM (103).
Drawn by H. P. Clifford.

* *History of the Cathedral*, 125.

Dawkes & Partridge, Photo.]

THE WEST FRONT.

be," as if they were felt to be mere interruptions to the lines of sculpture.

This latter objection to the doorways had often been made before, only that the " rabbit-holes on a mountain side " of earlier critics became " mouse-holes " with Mr Freeman. Mr E. W. Godwin, in a lecture in 1862, had also found fault with the crowding in of the niches over the central doorway, which he declared to be in the highest degree clumsy ; with the bald appearance given by the shallowness of the reveals in the principal windows ; and with the way in which " the solid work of the base suddenly crops up at the very summit of the two central buttresses, not altogether unlike the dog - kennel of modern Gothic."

Of these criticisms the most serious is Mr Freeman's general charge of unreality. But why should not a stone screen be erected for the display of statuary before the west end of a church, just as lawfully as behind the high altar ? And, if a screen may be allowed as an end in itself, standing simply as a thing of beauty to glorify a building of which it is not a structural part, then the front of Wells may stand, like the reredos of Winchester, as the noblest example of its kind. It has no need to simulate lofty aisles which do not exist, for it covers, not the aisles, but the faces of the great towers themselves ; and, as a consequence, the portion of really blank wall which stretches from them to the central gable is so small as to be more than justified by the cohesion it gives to the whole. The whole effect is singularly broad, but so is the space it covers within ; for this breadth is legitimately attained by the happy device of planting the western towers beyond the aisles.

The massive front of Wells stands, therefore, on its own merits as a west front, and not merely a west end—a great stone screen that, so far from pretending to be a regular termination of the nave and aisles, is actually carried, in all its sculptured magnificence, round the sides of the two towers upon which it so frankly depends. It is a screen built at a period different from, and, we may now safely assume, later than, that of the nave, and built for the exhibition of a noble legend in stone, which has ever since been the glory of a county famed for its splendid churches.

Taking it then for what it is, and remembering that the

lower tiers were once filled with statuary, can we regret that the doorways themselves were subordinated to the one grand design of accommodating this great multitude of silent teachers? The great doorways of French churches are magnificent in themselves, but that is surely no reason why we should make it an axiom that a front cannot be fine unless it have a great doorway. Striking as the effect of these foreign entrances may be, there is no structural reason why a door should be of an unwieldy size out of all proportion to the stature of the people who use it, so that a smaller door has to be cut for ordinary use out of the real door. It certainly, as even at Amiens, limits the sculptor's opportunities; and in a country like England, where doors can only be kept open for a few weeks in the year, great doorways would be as inappropriate as closed doors are forbidding. As a matter of fact, the usual entrance to Wells Cathedral in Jocelin's time was not from the west, but through the cloister and the south porch. And the central entrance of the west was made impressive, not by its size, but by the exquisite nature of its carving, and the blue and scarlet and gold with which it was coloured. It was not insignificant then. It had the prominence of a jewel. Moreover, in French churches, where the exterior is sacrificed to the internal effect, there is some wisdom in concentrating attention upon the doorway. But in English churches—and in Wells, perhaps, more than any other English church—the exteriors are perfect in themselves, and the visitor need not be tempted to hurry to their portals. After all, if the rabbit-holes on a mountain-side looked as large as quarries, the mountain would not look like a mountain.

There are, moreover, three faults in the front as it now stands which cannot be attributed to its maker. In the first place, it is undoubtedly a little formal, a little square, and this defect is particularly marked in the photographs which one sees everywhere. Unfortunately this picture, which is too small to show the detail, gives no idea whatever of the general external effect of the church. It gives the impression that Wells Cathedral is a glorified wall, because the photograph cannot show the other parts upon which the front depends. The architect, no doubt, intended the towers to be carried higher or surmounted with spires, and though no trace of any stone erection has been found on the tops of the present towers, they may once have been crowned with wooden spires covered with lead or shingle. One need hardly say how vast a difference such lofty towers as exist at Laon Cathedral, or spires like those of Lichfield, would make in the effect of the front. They would also account for the great size of the buttresses, which seem to have been built with a view to sustaining a great weight.

A disagreeable impression is also caused by the row of hip-knobs along the coping of the central gable, and the pinnacle in their midst. This collection of curiosities was probably added in the seventeenth century, and the pinnacle may have been taken from one of the denuded buttresses of the Lady Chapel to replace the gable cross which must have originally stood here : at all events it is a later addition, as was proved by an examination of the masonry. It would be an act of justice to the memory of Jocelin if these trivial excrescences were removed.

Perhaps one is even more distressed on first seeing the front by a third fault—the weak and stringy effect of the long, thin, dark, marble shafts. For this the restorer, Mr Benjamin Ferrey, must bear the blame. He complained with justice that the original blue lias shafts, when they were decayed, had been replaced by the ordinary Doulting stone.* But, unhappily, he did not go back to the original material, but fitted the whole front with a complete set of shafts of Kilkenny marble, which is at once dark and cold. They absolutely refuse to blend with the old, warm, grey stone, and stand out, stark and stiff, like an array of gigantic slate pencils. Mr Ferrey was possessed with the idea that the blue lias shafts (having only lasted for a paltry half-dozen centuries) were not durable enough for the work. He therefore used this marble, which, doubtless, will stand in increased obtrusiveness when every stone of the cathedral has decayed. He further was impressed with the strange notion that the hideous Kilkenny marble is of the same colour as the exquisitely delicate grey

---

* The Doulting stone, of which the cathedral is built, comes from the St. Andrew's quarry at the little village of Doulting, where Bishop Ealdhelm died. It is inferior oolite, and very like Bath stone, which is the greater oolite. The exterior shafts were blue lias, and those within either blue lias or Purbeck marble, though there are one or two shafts of red Draycot stone in the western responds of the nave.

of the blue lias. The result is a sad warning to all restorers not to be more clever than the original architect.

Let us, then, try to imagine the west front with its empty lowest tier filled with graceful figures, its gable in its first simplicity and surmounted by a cross, its towers of Early English form crowned with lofty spires, its delicate shafts of their original material, and its ranges of figures "all gorgeous in their freshly-painted hues of blue and scarlet and purple

ORNAMENTS IN THE WEST FRONT.

and gold." Then we shall have some idea of the front of Wells as Jocelin meant it to be and to remain.

As for the colour, its effect can be gathered from the traces which survive. There is ultramarine, gold, and scarlet in the tympanum of the central doorway, where there are also the marks of metal fitttings. Ferrey found a deep maroon colour on the figures of the Apostles, and a dark colour painted with stars in the Resurrection tier. One of the chief glories of the front is the faithful care which is given throughout to the smaller features. The mouldings (a succession of rounds and

hollows) are most bold and effective; the carving of the
foliage in caps and canopies, tympana, pedestals, and ter-
minals is singularly beautiful and free.   This impression
is deepened by a minute examination; indeed, it is almost
a matter of regret that some of the finest work is at such
a height as to be almost impossible to see; for in all the
earlier work at Wells the Lamp of Sacrifice burns brightly.
Mr Ferry pointed out an instance, which may be given here,
of the care with which minor matters were thought out:—In
order that the lowest tier might not look weak and yet might
provide a sufficient shadow for the statues, the backs of the

ORNAMENTS IN THE WEST FRONT.

niches are set at a slightly recessed angle in the centre,
and thus an effect of strength is given to the angular jambs.
Indeed, there may be differences of opinion as to the general
design of the west front, but there can be none as to the
supreme excellence of its detail.   It is beyond doubt the most
rich example of Early English work to be found anywhere.
The crown of its glories, the justification of its form, did it need
justification, are the frail statues which line it, tier upon tier.
    Vertically the west front is divided into three main parts—
the centre, containing the three lancet windows of the nave
and the main doorway, is surmounted by a gable receding in
stages with a pinnacle at either angle; and the two lateral
towers, the lower portion of which form one continuous screen

with the centre, broken only by the boldly projecting buttresses, of which each division possesses two. Horizontally the front divides itself naturally into four parts—the plain base, which is high enough to contain the full height of the small north and south doorways. One of the stones in this division, about the level of the eye, and near the middle, which has evidently been moved from some other place, bears the inscription, *Pur lalme Johan de Putenie priez et trieze jurs de* . . . Next is an arcade of niches interspersed with windows, the space above being pierced by quatrefoils. The third division contains the three lancet windows, the forms of which are repeated on the north and south, breaking the line of the two historical tiers of niches which, with the Resurrection tier, adorn this main division of the front. A bold string course marks it off firmly and decisively from the fourth and upper division, in which the three parts of the front become separate, the towers at each side and the stepped gable, flanked by two graceful Early English pinnacles, in the middle. The statuary is mainly confined to the arcading of the second division, to the buttresses of the third, with its continuous cornice of the Resurrection tier, and to the gable front of the fourth; but the amount of it is largely increased by the fact that the work is carried round three sides of the north-western tower, which only touches the church on one side. The niches on the sides of the south-western tower are almost empty.

The Statuary.—The statuary is not only the finest collection of medieval sculpture to be found in England; but, separately, the figures are with few exceptions finer than any others in this country, while some of them are almost as beautiful as the greatest masterpieces in Italy or France. It is strange that here, at the outset of the Gothic period, the chief characteristics of the old Greek spirit should be so apparent, the same restraint, the same simplicity, the same exquisite appreciation of light and flowing drapery: in other things there is difference enough, the form is less perfect, the action is less free, though there is a deeper sentiment and a higher power of spiritual expression; but in the essentials of sublime statuary there is a singular agreement.

And, strange though it seems, it may well be that in these statues one must look for the first signs of the influence of the Renaissance in England. Romanesque work has but just died out, and already the old spirit, destined in time to supplant the architecture which sprung from it, is at work again. While the statues were being cut at Wells, Niccola Pisano was reviving sculpture in Italy under the inspiration of classical examples ; and there can be little doubt but that it was Italian sculptors who produced the statuary at Wells. Some of the figures on the northern part of the front have been found to be marked with Arabic numerals (*Somerset Proceedings* 1888, i. 57, 62), and these numerals, which did not become common in England till the sixteenth century, were used in Italy long before, having been introduced by Bonacci of Pisa (a fellow-citizen of Niccola) in 1202. That they are found here before the middle of the century is a fairly conclusive proof that the workers were Italians, and very likely from Pisa itself. Jocelin, indeed, was English, but he had been in exile from 1208 to 1213, when he had ample opportunity of studying the work of the Italian artists. Pleasant as it would be to our national pride, we can hardly believe that Englishmen produced what sems to be the earliest example of such magnificent and varied sculpture in north-western Europe. At Jocelin's death, in 1242, when the work had been going on for some thirty years, Niccola Pisano was in his prime, Cimabue was two years

WEST FRONT : CHRISTINA (185).
Drawn by H. P. Clifford.

old, and forty years had yet to elapse before the rival sculpture of Amiens Cathedral was executed.

Mr Ruskin, whose admiration of the work at Amiens is so intense, has given almost as high praise to the sculpture at Wells, and has presented sets of photographs of the statuary to various art schools. The verdict of enthusiastic approval is, in fact, unanimous. Flaxman, to his credit, in spite of his classicalism, was one of the first to draw attention to the work. Whoever was the general designer of the whole arrangement, he deserves as great praise as the sculptors themselves. There must have been several sculptors, both because no one man could have carved three hundred and fifty subjects (of which one hundred and fifty-two are life-size or colossal), and because a certain number of the figures in the fourth and fifth tiers are of obviously inferior design. But one master-mind must have conceived and directed the work. The height and lightness which is given to the gable by the tall row of the Apostles, the solemn prominence of the figure of our Lord above, the rich cornice-like effect of the small Resurrection tier, the difference in height between the fourth and fifth tiers, the concentration of the three lower tiers, the breadth which the seated figures give to the face of the buttresses, the arrangement of the statues and groups round the buttresses, which makes it impossible for them all to be seen at once, all show that one mind was busy, carefully subordinating the parts to the whole.

It may well have been Jocelin himself who planned the subject-matter of the statuary with such admirable breadth and balance of mind. It is easy to produce sermons in stones, easy to sermonise in very many ways; but Jocelin did not preach. He just tried to embody the Christian spirit at work in the world: God made manifest in man, the great truth of the Incarnation; and this he did in what we should call the most modern manner, though in truth it is medieval as well as modern. He did not conceive of Christianity as confined within the covers of the Bible, but he took all history, as he knew it, the patient education of man in the Old Testament, the fulfilment of man's aspirations and God's purpose in the New, from the birth of our Lord to the founding of the Church, and the continuation of this church up to his own time, with especial regard to the heroes, saints and rulers of the Church of England. He made a "kalendar for unlearned men," which is both a *Biblia Pauperum* and *Annales Angliae,* because the annals of England were to him a new Bible. "Slowly the Bible of the race is writ," a modern writer has said, "each age, each kindred, adds a word to it." That was the spirit of Jocelin's design; only that, through the pomp of mighty kings and fair women and honoured bishops, he looked to the naked truth of the judgment time, when mitres and crowns would remain but as signs of an awful responsibility, and the divine justice, so tried, so obscured on earth, would be vindicated before the angels who are quick to do God's will, and the twelve plain men who turned the mighty currents of the world. Such was the spirit of a man who lived in the days of St. Francis and St. Louis, Stephen Langton and Roger Bacon.

Before commencing a detailed description of the statuary, one must refer to Professor Cockerell, R.A., whose enthusiastic love of the work led him to construct a theory which he published in 1851, as an *Iconography of the West Front*. There can be little doubt that he was right in his general idea; there can be equally little doubt that he was wrong in nearly every application of it. Everyone now, for instance, takes it for granted that the south side of the front is mainly " spiritual," devoted to ecclesiastics, while the north is "temporal "; and that the whole of the fourth and fifth tiers do represent certain leading historical figures. But when we read Cockerell's reasons for identifying these figures we recoil in dismay. His knowledge of history is superficial, of costume he knows practically nothing; his drawings are as inaccurate as his imagination is fertile, and he states as obvious facts the wildest conjectures. Further reference will be found to his book in our description of the fourth and fifth tiers. It was at least an honest labour of love, and Cockerell deserves the honour, as he had to endure the disadvantages, of being the first in the field.

The **central doorway** may be taken before the lowest tier. Its soffit contains an evident addition, as if the architect felt that it needed emphasising by some enrichment. In the first of its four deeply-wrought mouldings a series of niches, five on each side, with small delicately-carved figures, has been inserted, evidently after the arch was made; they are cut from a different stone (white lias), and are skilfully fitted and grooved into the back of the large sunk moulding. They add considerably to the effect of the arch, although all the heads of the figures have been destroyed. It is characteristic of Cockerell's random method of conjecture, that he declared these figures to be representations of the Ten Commandments.

1. The tympanum under the arch and above the double opening of the doorway contains a quatrefoil, in which is a noble sculpture of the Madonna

and Child. The head of the Mother and the upper half of the Child are gone, but the drapery that remains is of quite perfect grace and dignity. A serpent is under the feet of the Madonna, who is sitting on a throne; angels censing are on either side without the quatrefoil. A good deal of the old colour which once gave this central group a peculiar brilliancy can still be traced on this protected sculpture; the background was ultra-marine, the mouldings red and gold. The figures were also gilded in part, and there are marks on the wall to show that a metal nimbus was once attached to it.

2. In a canopy above the arch is another sculpture of equal beauty, though, owing to its more exposed position, the treatment is a little broader. It represents the coronation of Our Lady; both the heads and all the hands are gone. The two figures are both seated on one long bench, and our Lord leans forward to place the crown upon his Mother's head.

THE TIERS.

In order to avoid any possible mistake I have taken each tier from right to left, specifying the gaps, windows, and buttresses, to facilitate identification, and commencing with the lowest tier. I have also numbered the figures afresh, because of the confusion which has hitherto caused great waste of time to every one who has attempted to identify them. Cockerell's numbers are the only ones that are at all accurate (and he omits the two figures on the extreme south of the fourth and fifth tiers); but, as he recommenced his enumeration with each series, they are not much use for purposes of identification. There are mistakes and omissions in the enumeration of the photographs, there are mistakes in the album in the cathedral library, the photographs in the South Kensington Museum are hopelessly muddled, and even the descriptions of the restorer, Mr Ferrey, are so arranged that it takes days to identify them, while some of them elude one's efforts altogether. I have, therefore, numbered the statues and groups in a continuous order from bottom to top, so that comparison with photographs will in the future be easy. In the case of work most of which can only be seen from a distance, the study of photographs is absolutely necessary for a full appreciation of their beauty, more especially as in very many cases the photographs reveal the form which the accidents of discoloration have partly concealed. Mr Phillips of 10 Market Place has an almost complete set of admirable photographs, which he was enabled to take when the scaffolding was up for the restoration of 1870-73: it is these which Mr Ruskin has so much admired.

As there are so many statues, some of inferior interest and beauty, I have ventured to put an asterisk (*) to those which I think no one should fail to see; and, in almost every case, I have but echoed the general verdict.

The Lowest Tier.—This tier contains sixty-two niches, forty-three of which are empty, so fatally convenient has their position been for the iconoclast. Of those which remain nearly all are on the north side of the tower, so that at first sight the tier seems to be quite empty. The loss here has been the greater because the figures were of the finest kind, as well as the most easily seen: those remaining are certainly of the most exquisite loveliness. Cockerell's theory that this tier represents the heralds of the gospel, prophets and missionaries, has nothing to support it.

It seems to me not unlikely that the tier was devoted to some of the most popular saints in the calendar; the position, so near the passer-by, would have suited this arrangement, and the front must have been singularly deficient in saints if it were otherwise. The figures which remain, a group of deacons, a group of bearded figures holding books, and of women bearing religious attributes, might well stand for saints.

3. *South Tower*. Male figure, much decayed, held by metal clamps.

4. Male figure, much decayed, held by metal clamps.
   Rest of figures missing along west front up to—

5. *North Tower*. Male figure, much decayed, holds book.

6. A similar figure.
   Missing.

7. *North Buttress*. Male figure, which held some drapery in front.

8. *North Buttress*. Male figure, holding a vessel in right hand covered with a cloth, the end of which was in left hand. [Cockerell calls this St. Augustine, erroneously supposing this cloth to be the pallium.]

9. Beautiful female figure,* drapery resembling a chasuble; hands gone.

10. Female figure with flowing hair; hands gone.

11. Female figure, wimple round head, in left hand holds a vessel, right hand is on the edge of the vessel, the fingers dipping in.

12. Female figure,* hood over head, holds in right hand the foot of a chalice, and with her left the fold of her dress in front.

13. Tall male figure, bearded, holding closed book; in good preservation.

14. Male figure, bearded; hands gone.

15. *Buttress*. Male figure, bearded, with flowing hair; hands gone.

16. *Buttress*. Male figure, bearded, holding open book in left hand; upper part moulding away.

17. Deacon* in dalmatic, alb, amice, holding open book in left hand, right hand gone; drapery is wonderfully fine. (This and the remaining figures are tonsured and shaven.)

18. Deacon,* a beautiful figure, (apparently in dalmatic), amice; left hand gone.

19. Deacon, in girded alb, ends of girdle hanging down, wears the folded chasuble (very rare in art) over left shoulder, maniple; holds book with both hands.
    Missing.

20. *Buttress*. Deacon, in girded alb, amice, stole over left shoulder, book in left hand. Besides ends of girdle, end of a stole is visible on left side, as if a crossed stole had first been carved and this end forgotten.

21. *Buttress*. Deacon,* stole worn over left shoulder, maniple, but no amice and no girdle; wears instead of alb a surplice with full sleeves—an unusual combination.

Second Tier.—The next tier (22-53) consists of thirty-two quatrefoils, some of which are now empty. The rest contain half-length figures of angels, holding crowns, mitres, scrolls, or drapery in their hands.

Third Tier.—This, which we may call the Bible Tier, consists of forty-eight quatrefoils, ranged close above the quatrefoils of the second tier, and broken in the centre by the larger sculpture of the Coronation of the Virgin (2). The subjects are all from the Bible, those on the south from the Old Testament, dealing with the first things, while those on the north and on the north and east sides of the northern tower are from the New Testament, and represent the life and mission of our Lord. The iconoclasts seem to have concentrated their attention on those earlier New Testament groups, which would contain the figure of our Lady, and they have made the Crucifixion almost unrecognisable. The figures are about two feet high.

Empty.

54. The Death of Jacob.
55. Isaac blessing Jacob, who leans over him.
56. Meeting of Isaac and Rebecca, probably.
57. Noah sacrificing on Ararat. Very fine.
58. The Ark. A curious structure, raised pyramidally in four tiers, with open arcades, in which birds and beasts are seen. Below is the Flood.
59. Noah building the Ark.* He is in workman's dress, and wears a cap ; he is working at a bench, beneath which are his tools. Behind is the ark, and an " Early English " tree.
60. God decreeing the Deluge.* In great wrath Jehovah approaches a man who sits pensively on a hill-side : from behind the man's head springs a demon. The figure of Jehovah is admirably expressed.

Empty.

61. Abraham about to sacrifice Isaac, who is bound on a bundle of wood. Cockerell called this the Sacrifice of Cain, which certainly suits its position better.
62. Adam delves and Eve spins. Fine.

Empty.

63. Jehovah in the Garden. A draped figure, addressing two figures naked and ashamed.

64. The Temptation. The serpent's body is coiled round the tree near Adam, and his head hovers above with an apple in the mouth. Adam is already eating the fruit.
65. God placing Adam and Eve in the Garden of Eden.
66. The Creation of Eve.
67. The Creation of Adam. The figure of the Almighty in each of these three is magnificent, especially in the last.

Empty.

Over central doorway. 2. Coronation of the Virgin (p. 34).

Here follow eighteen New Testament subjects.

68. St. John the Evangelist * ; he is winged. A book rests on the back of an eagle. The idea of inspiration could not be more finely expressed.
   Empty. (Perhaps the Annunciation was here.)
   Empty. (Perhaps the Visitation.)
69. The Nativity. Mutilated.
   Empty.
   Empty.
   Empty.
   Empty.
   Empty.
   Empty.
70. Christ among the Doctors : the Holy Child is a very small figure on a pedestal. A most expressive group.
71. St. John Baptist, clothed in camels' hair, in the wilder-

ness. (An angel appearing from the clouds, broken off since 1862. The fragment is now in No. 72).

72. Figures in critical attitudes. Perhaps the Sermon on the Mount.
Empty.

73. Christ in the Wilderness, probably.

74. Figures in intent attitudes. Perhaps the Mission of the Apostles.

75. Five figures seated at a table. Perhaps the Anointing of Christ's feet.

76. Figure on a Mount surrounded by many figures. Perhaps the Feeding of the Five Thousand.

North side of Tower.

77. Christ, sitting, with other figures. Perhaps the Feeding of the Four Thousand.

78. The Transfiguration.* A fine composition, two of the Apostles crouching in the foreground.

79. The Entry into Jerusalem. Under the city gate two men strew clothes and branches :

from the walls and tower many people are looking.

80. The Betrayal. Chief priest with mitred head-dress in centre : winged devil holds up the train of right figure. On left a figure holds open a money-box.

81. The Last Supper.* The Virgin kneels to receive the Communion from her Son : St. John's head rests on His bosom. The drapery is very fine. Underneath are a bottle and a basket.
Empty.

82. Christ before Pilate.

83. Christ bearing the Cross. Mutilated.

84. The Elevation of the Cross. Much mutilated.

85. The Deposition. Much mutilated.
Empty.

86. The Resurrection. An angel on either side, guards below.

87. Pentecost : the Birthday of Holy Church. A dignified group of figures.

Fourth and Fifth Tiers.—The fourth and fifth tiers contained at least 120 figures (about a dozen of which are gone), varying in height from 7 ft. 10 in. to 8 ft. 1 in., a few running as high as 8 ft. 10 in. They no doubt represent the kings, bishops, and heroes of English history from Egbert to Henry II. Cockerell was probably right in his general interpretation of the series, but it is easy to prove that he is wrong in many of the names he gives. It is not so easy to suggest any better, and therefore his names have stuck to the figures, since people naturally like to know them by something more interesting than a number. I shall therefore adopt his nomenclature, with the admission that equally good grounds could be given in almost every case for some other theory. Besides Mr Ferrey's account (*Inst. Brit. Arch.*, 1870), quoted in inverted commas, Cockerell's descriptions, inaccurate as they are, have been consulted, and also Mr Planché's criticism of Cockerell.

The word *Buttress* means that the figure (generally a sitting one) is on the west face of the buttress in question. Bishops (" Bp. "), unless otherwise stated, wear the usual vestments—mitre, chasuble, dalmatic, tunicle, stole, maniple, alb, and apparelled amice. Kings (" K. ") and Queens (" Q. ") wear crowns. A favourite attitude is described as " holding cord " ; this cord being the lace or cord of the mantle, which crossed the chest and prevented that garment from falling off the shoulders. The mantle seems to have had an uncomfortable tendency to slip down, and thus it became a habit constantly to pull the cord forward, whence the frequency of this attitude. This cord was wrongly described by Cockerell as a necklace, with which it has, of course, no connection. The word "trampling" refers to another common feature in these tiers; kings are generally represented as trampling on a small figure under their feet, to signify their success over their enemies. The figures of the fifth tier are rather taller than those of the fourth. The first twenty figures on our list, those of the fourth tier up to King Ina, may represent the twenty bishops of the diocese from Athelm to Jocelin, in direct order, since the corresponding series of the fifth tier contains figures which cannot be those of bishops. I have, however, kept to Cockerell's names to avoid confusion.

Fourth Tier.— 88. *South Tower —Buttress*—Sitting Bp.; much decayed, supported by metal clamps.

89. Bp. Savaric. Much defaced, head grotesquely so.

90. Bp. Robert. Much defaced, head grotesquely.
Missing.

91. *Buttress.* Bp. Reginald de Bohun, sitting; somewhat decayed.

92. Bp. Ethelweard, good drapery, well - preserved; no hair or beard.

93. Sighelm, good drapery, well-preserved; ring of curly hair and beard.

94. Alfry, in hood; large curly beard.

95. Etheleage, monastic dress, cowl and scapular; large curly beard.

96. Bp. Asser. Short and stout figure, in attitude of benediction.

97. Bp. Heahmund. Short and stout figure, in attitude of benediction.

98. *Buttress.* Bp. Wolfhelm. Fine seated figure, in attitude of benediction.

99. Bp. Ealhstan. Stout commonplace figure; rather mutilated.

100. Bp. Wilbert. Stout commonplace figure; rather mutilated.

101. Bp. Denefrith. Stout commonplace figure; better preserved.

102. Bp. Ethelnod. Stout commonplace figure; better preserved.

103. *Buttress.* Bp. Aethelhelm, first Bishop of Wells * (reproduced on p. 22). Noble figure, sitting in attitude of benediction.

104. Bp. Herewald, in attitude of benediction.

105. Bp. Forthere, head bent slightly forward.

106. Bp. Ealdhelm. A fine figure.
Central Window (South).

107. K. Ina, looking over right shoulder, hand gone. (These central figures, Ina and Ethelburga, are supposed to be of later date than the rest.)
Central Window.

108. Q. Ethelburga. Wears the long kirtle with girdle, from which are hung an ink-bottle and aulmoniere.
Central Window (North).

109. K. Egbert, trampling, bearded; cloak falls in a graceful sweep from right to left.

110. K. Ethelwulf, bearded. A very short figure, but raised on high stone (crouching figure ?) higher than the others.

111. K. Ethelbald; decayed.

112. *Buttress.* K. Edgar, sitting, flat cap on head.

113. K. Ethelbert, smooth face, trampling; apparently holds fragment of sceptre in right hand, cord of mantle with left.

114. K. Ethelred I., smooth face, trampling, gracefully draped cloak, holds fragment of sceptre apparently in right, and something indistinct in left hand.

115. K. Edwy, left arm raised, holding cloak, which is over right shoulder.

116. K. Edward the Martyr, bearded, holding cup (his usual symbol) in left hand, trampling. This is one of the most likely ascriptions.

117. *Buttress.* K. Edmund, sitting, right arm uplifted, left resting on knee. Fast decaying.

118. K. Ethelred the Unready, bearded, short figure, trampling, but the trampled figure leans easily on its elbow.

119. K. Cnut, bearded, short figure, trampling, but the trampled figure is apparently still struggling.

120. Q. Osburga,* in long supertunic, with ample sleeves, falling in folds over the feet. The tight sleeve of her kirtle appears on left arm, which holds cord of mantle. Head and neck in the wimple which was not in thirteenth century distinctive of nun's dress. Book in right hand.

121. Q. Emma, in flowing supertunic with ample sleeves, and wimple; hands gone.

122. Harold I., no head covering, trampling; hands touching girdle.

123. Harthacnut, like Harold, but hands and part of face gone.

124. *Buttress.* K. Edred, sitting, right hand on knee, left raised to cord, drapery crossed.

125. Q. Edgitha, mantle falls round over left foot.

126. Edmund Ironside.* Knight in surcoat over chain armour, hauberk but no helmet; right arm and left hand gone, but head turned to left and attitude is that of drawing or sheathing his sword.

127. Harold. Knight, hauberk and surcoat of mail, cylindrical helmet, shield on left side; delapidated.

128. *North Side of Tower. Buttress.* Edward the Confessor, in cap; sitting in attitude of judgment (Planché), left hand resting on right ankle, this leg being crossed over left knee.

129. Prince Richard.* Crowned figure of great beauty, bearded, head slightly bent to left with a melancholy expression; hands gone.

130. Robert Curthouse,* bearded, the right hand draws aside part of the surcoat, exposing right leg in curious hose; left leg covered by surcoat.

131. K. Rufus,* bearded, right hand holds cord of mantle, left holds border of mantle across his body.

132. Q. Matilda, flowing hair, holds mantle in left hand.

133. Emperor Henry, crowned, holds cord of mantle, with right hand fingering end of his girdle.

134. K. Stephen, right hand holds cord of mantle, left on girdle.

135. K. Henry II., end of cloak thrown over shoulder, holds the fold with both hands; in good preservation.

136. *Buttress.* K. William the Conqueror, sitting in menac-

ing attitude, elbows projecting, and hands upon knees.

137. Prince Henry. A dignified
figure; hands gone.

138. Prince Geoffrey. Beautiful
figure, head gone, holds cord
of mantle, loose sleeves, and
good drapery. (Ferrey is wrong
in calling this a female figure.)

139. Q. Maude the Good, flowing
hair, left hand on girdle of
supertunic, dress fastened at
neck with "a beautiful jewel"
(Ferrey).

140. Adelais. Graceful figure, with
flowing hair.

141. *Buttress.* K. Henry I., sitting in defiant attitude, right
arm akimbo, left knee raised,
foot on pedestal.
Missing.
Missing.
Missing.

142. K. John.* A beautiful figure.

143. Henry III., no crown, standing, but right knee raised to
suit the weathering of aisle
roof.

Fifth Tier.—144. *South Tower.*
Buttress on the south side.
Sitting Bp., supported by
metal clamps.

145. Bp. J. de Villula; hands gone,
much decayed, clamped.

146. Bp. Gisa ; hands gone.

147. Bp. Duduc* ; right hand gone,
book in left.

148. *Buttress.* Bp. Lyfing; decayed.

149. Bp. Merewit ; hands gone.

150. Bp. Brihtwine ; hands gone.

151. Aethelwine. Fine figure with
long wavy beard spreading at
end, hood and mantle, aulmoniere at girdle.

152. Burwold, tall bearded figure
in hood, satchel (?) hanging
from girdle.

153. Bp. Aelfwine.* Beautiful figure
in cowl, curly hair and beard,
finely draped habit with
loose sleeves.

154. Bp. Sigegar, book in left hand.

155. *Buttress.* Bp. Brithelm, head
turned to right; decayed.

156. Bp. Cyneward.

157. Bp. Wulfhelm. A fine figure.

158. Bp. Elfege. A fine figure.

159. Edfleda, flowing hair, in
supertunic or surcoat with
long and wide sleeves, head
covered with veil, which
hangs behind, no wimple.
Nothing conventual to suggest
Edfleda.

160. *Buttress.* K. Edward the
Elder. Fine figure, right hand
on knees, left on cord of
mantle.
Missing.

161. Edgitha. Very tall figure, right
hand on cord, left holds end
of veil.
Missing.
Central Window (South).

162. Q. Edgiva, kirtle only, with
crown and veil, no wimple.
Central Window.

163. Ethilda. Wears supertunic
over her kirtle, veil and
wimple.
Central Window (North).

164. Hugh. A sword hangs from
his girdle on left side.

165. Elgiva.

166. Q. Edgiva ; hands gone.

167. *Buttress.* K. Ethelstan,
defiant attitude, right foot on
stool, wears brooch.

168. K. Charles the Simple. A
squat figure with very big
head, trampling.

169. Otho, close - fitting tunic,
over which is mantle with
handsome fastening.
Missing.

170. Guthrum. Knight in surcoat,
mail hauberk and chausses,
shield on left side.

171. *Buttress.* K. Alfred, seated ;
both hands gone, front decayed, and clamped.

172. Earl of Mercia.* Knight in

helmet with cross-slit, holding right hand up and shield upon left arm; the surcoat turned over below the waist shows a suit of mail. Well preserved.

173. St. Neot (more probably St. Decuman, as St. Neot was not beheaded). Bp. holding with both hands the upper part of his head, which has been cut off across the brows.

174. Ethelfleda,* the Lady of the Mercians. A striking and beautiful figure with flowing hair, long veil hanging below the waist, supertunic held by brooch, but without sleeves, the tight sleeves of her kirtle being visible to the shoulders.

175. Ethelward. Woman with flowing hair, veil; hands gone.

176. Grimbald. Priest; hands gone.

177. St. Elfege, Archb.; hands gone; a noble figure.

178. *Buttress.* St. Dunstan, upper part decayed.

179. Turketul. Short figure, trampling, in very pointed cloak, big head in cap.

180. John Scotus.* A beautiful figure, with exquisitively fine drapery that looks as thin as gauze.
Missing.

181. *North Side of Tower.— Buttress.* Robert, Archbishop of Canterbury, standing, holding book in right hand, left hand gone; no mitre.

182. Q. Elgiva, drapery falls from left shoulder, is folded over right arm; book in left hand.

183. Q. Edgitha. Tall, gaunt figure; veil falls in long folds to knee, right arm close to side, left hand holds cord.

184. Q. Edburga, circlet round head, brooch on her breast, holds drapery in right hand.
Missing.

Missing.

185. Christina, Abbess of Romsey.* Beautiful female figure, holding box in left hand: "her dress is peculiar": one end of veil is caught over right shoulder, the other falls down in front on right side (p. 31).

186. Wulston of Winchester, bearded, "with distended ears"; right hand gone.

187. *Buttress.* Archb. Aldred of York, sitting; "mitre modern," it is conical in shape.

188. Edgar Atheling. Knight, spurred, in surcoat only, with sword girded outside, no mail, but close-fitting cap and fillet on head: the fillet was used for the large cylindrical helmet to rest on. He carries what may be a palmer's hat (Cockerell points out that Edgar went on a pilgrimage); but Planché says it must be a small Saxon buckler, as pilgrims did not carry swords. It certainly looks like a hat.

189. Robert the Saxon. Knight in hauberk, without mail, but feet spurred, cap on head, shield and sword.

190. Falk of Anjou. Knight in hauberk and chausses of mail, hood of hauberk enclosing whole head except a portion of the face: on head is the thick fillet. He covers his body with a shield. His surcoat is deeply jagged.

191. Robert of Normandy. Knight, in hauberk and complete suit of mail, in good preservation, shield with boss on it held down: he wears cylindrical helmet, his eyes and nose being visible through the slit.

192. *Buttress.* B. Roger of Salisbury, sitting, without mitre.

Missing.
Missing.

193. Female figure, holding drapery with right arm, left hand on side.

194. St. Nicholas, the patron saint of baptism, stands in water up to knees, holding a child in each arm. This ascription is approved by Planché. (He is commonly called by children "the pancake man," the conventional water suggesting round cakes).

195. Female figure, in good preservation, but clamped in a sloping position, drapery good.

The Resurrection Tier.—The sixth tier (195-283) consists of a series of small canopies which run continuously under the cornice that finishes the main division of the front. Above and around, the spandrels are filled with beautiful foliage most boldly undercut. Each of the eighty-eight canopies (of which thirty are on the north side) contains a figure, or group of figures, representing the Resurrection of the dead. In spite of a rather defective anatomy, these figures are singularly impressive, "startling in significance, pathos, and expression," are Cockerell's words. They are naked—crowns, mitres, and tonsures alone remaining to distinguish their office. They awaken by degrees, heave up the lids of their tombs, and draw themselves up slowly, as if scarcely yet awake. Some sit in a strange dreamy posture with folded arms, some seem expectant, others are in attitudes of fear, hope, defiance, and despair. There are none of the grotesque accessories which are too common in ancient representations of this subject, but the awful feeling of a great awakening shivers along this range of naked, grey, stone figures. It is probably the earliest representation of the subject in art ; it is certainly the most profound and spiritual.

The Angels' Tier.—This is immediately above the Resurrection Tier, and occupies the lower part of the gable only. The angelic figures stand in nine low niches with well-moulded trefoil heads that rested on blue lias shafts ; the two niches on the returns of the buttresses also contain angels, which are represented as blowing trumpets. In all probability the nine figures symbolise the nine orders of the heavenly hierarchy, and I have ventured to give the names which the attributes and position suggest to my mind as the most likely. Mr Ferrey's account is quoted in inverted commas : it must be remembered that he had the advantage of a close inspection from the scaffolding.

284. Thrones. "Angel holding an open book," two wings, long robe, facing to his right.

285. Cherubim. "Seraph," with four wings, "apparently holding a banner," decayed.

286. Seraphim. "Seraph," with four wings, "entirely feathered, with bare legs and feet," face gone.

287. Dominations. "Angel wearing a helmet," in vigorous attitude, two wings, "too dilapidated to make out what its attributes are."

288. (*Central Figure*). Powers. "Beautifully robed, holding a sceptre," two wings : the dress is very ample and majestic.

289. Virtues. "Robed in a short tunic, with an ornamental border, the legs are encased in armour," wears "a jewelled cap," two wings.

290. Principalities. "A Seraph,

entirely feathered, holding a vessel shaped like a bowl," with flames issuing out of it, the legs and feet being also enveloped in "wavy lines of flames: probably the avenging angel"; four wings.

291. Archangels. "Apparently holding a crown in the right and left hands, close to his breast," long robe covering the feet; two wings.

292. Angels. "Carrying a regal or small hand organ," in left hand, four wings, decayed; apparently bearing a wand in right hand.

The Apostles' Tier.—The next tier, that of the Apostles, who are thus raised above the angels, contains twelve figures of imposing design, later in style than the rest of the statuary. The figures are hollowed out at the back so as to press less heavily on the tier beneath. The arrangement of these niches is very happily managed, so as to avoid any monotony in the range of twelve similar niches; for, besides the natural division formed by the small attached shafts between the figures, an additional projecting shaft in every third division forms the tier into four large bays with three figures in each. The capitals of these niches are remarkable, the graceful foliage being disposed in a very free manner, in some cases growing upwards, in others bent down, but always true to the outline of the capital. Of the figures themselves the central one, in the place of honour, and taller than the rest, is St. Andrew. The others are not all so easy to name, the attributes of some having disappeared; and, although Cockerell gave names to them all (some of which were certainly wrong), we may content ourselves with the following list, which at least is accurate so far as it goes:—

293. No symbol in hand, which is covered with drapery. (Carter's drawing represents a staff or spear, but he is quite unreliable, though it is occasionally possible that the attributes he draws did exist when he saw the figures a century ago.

294. Book (?) in right hand, a vessel or bag of cylindrical form is apparently suspended from the left arm. Perhaps St. Matthew with his purse.

295. Holds something, which may be the fuller's club, in which case the figure is that of St. James the Less; forked beard.

296. Club (?) in hand, long curly hair and beard. There is something near the knee, which may be a palmer's hat. (Carter drew this figure as St. Bartholomew with knife and skin.)

297. Carter drew this figure as St. Peter with the keys.

298. St. Andrew with his cross; he is so tall that his head fills the upper portion of the canopy.

299. St. John holding the chalice, which has large bowl and short stem; wavy hair. This is the only figure not bearded.

300. St. James the Greater. Staff in right hand, large satchel on left side hung from hand over right shoulder, book in left hand (the book of the Gospels with which St. James is always represented, in addition to the pilgrim's stiff and scrip). He wears a high cap.

301. Perhaps St. Paul (who is often represented among the

Twelve), with sword and book.

302. St. Philip holds drapery in right hand. Ferrey says the five loaves can be distinguished.

303. Long hair and head-dress like a veil bound by a fillet round the brows, forked beard, book in left hand, girdle.

304. This figure occasioned much controversy, owing to Carter having drawn it with a crown. Cockerell therefore attributed it to St. Peter, and said that the crown showed Bishop Jocelin's papistical tendencies! Planché scoffed at this, remarking with truth that none of the Apostles are ever represented with crowns, but he caused even greater confusion by suggesting that the figure stood for a Saxon king, and that the tier, in spite of the Apostolic number, did not represent the twelve Apostles. If he had looked at the actual figures instead of Carter's drawings he would have seen that there is no crown at all. In the photographs this is still clearer, the Apostle's head being evidently covered by nothing more imposing than his own long hair or a veil like that of the preceding figure.

The Uppermost Tier.—The whole magnificent series was fitly crowned by this group (305), of which only the lower part of the central figure remains. That, however, sufficiently attests the noble character of the rest : it represents our Lord seated in glory within a vesica-shaped niche. The feet are pierced. It seems to have been mutilated by Monmouth's followers, for it still bears the marks of their bullets. The two figures in the niches on either side must also have been destroyed at this time, for they are shown in a print in Dugdale's *Monasticon*. Ferrey cannot have seen this print when he suggested that the figures were of angels censing, for they are there given as representing Our Lady (new covenant) and John Baptist (old covenant).

The Western Towers.

—The projection of these towers beyond the aisles of the nave gives its great breadth to the west front, which is 147 feet across, as against the 116 feet of the almost contemporary cathedral of Amiens, which is twice its height. It is an unusual arrangement, of which there is no exactly similar example except at Rouen. Above the screen the towers are Perpendicular, the southern tower having been completed towards the end of the fourteenth, and the northern at the beginning of the fifteenth century. They are thus later additions to the original design of the front, and make it more difficult for us to realise the effect that was first intended.

These two towers are very nearly alike, but the southern, or Harewell, tower is some forty years the earlier of the two, and belongs to the earliest days of the Perpendicular style, Bishop Harewell having died in 1386. The northern tower was built

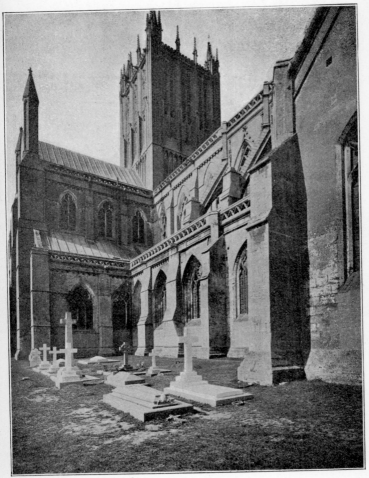

THE CENTRAL TOWER: FROM THE SOUTH-EAST.

with a sum of money left for the purpose by Bishop Bubwith, who died in 1424, and his arms are carved high up on a buttress upon the north side, those on the west being a modern copy. In one of its two western niches is a figure of the bishop in prayer. Both the towers have two belfry windows on each side, tiny battlements, and a stair-turret on the outer western angle ; in both the buttresses are carried up, with but slight reduction in bulk, two-thirds of their height and then finished with small pinnacles. There are, however, certain slight differences between the two towers ; their height is not exactly equal, and there are no niches on the earlier one. The south tower contains a peal of eight bells ; that on the north is traditionally considered "rotten," but to all appearance it is sound enough.

The Central Tower is Early English to the level of the roof. The two upper stages are Decorated, but there is a curious inter-mixture of styles in them, owing to the repairs that were made after the settlements of 1321. The chapter seemed determined to allow no possibility of another accident, for besides the inverted arches and buttresses of the interior, the original high narrow windows of the upper part of the tower have been fortified by later insertions, by way of bonding and stiffening the structure, which had been so endangered by the sinking of its piers below. There are, however, no signs of any rents in the Decorated part. The tower has square angular turrets, and is divided vertically into three main compartments, each division being marked by a small pinnacle, and the turrets by large compound pinnacles. It is an interesting tower to ascend, the rents in the wall being plainly discernible ; and from the summit there is a fine view of Wells and of the valley in which the city stands.

The **North Porch** is perhaps the finest piece of architecture at Wells, though it generally receives far less attention than it deserves. It is certainly the oldest part of the church, and must have been the first work which Bishop Reginald undertook, about 1185 ; in style it retains much of the Norman influence. The mouldings of the noble entrance arch are numerous and bold, and twice the Norman zig-zag occurs, though enriched with leaves in a manner that suggests the coming Gothic. A weather moulding, exquisitely carved with deeply undercut foliage, covers the arch. Its capitals on the east side contain figures among their leaves representing the martyrdom of St. Edmund the King: the first three of the caps have the saint in the midst, crowned, and transfixed with a number of conventionally-arranged arrows, and his enemies, two on either side, drawing their bows; the fourth cap shows an executioner cutting off the saint's head; in the fifth the head is found by the wolf; the sixth has been partly cut away, but the body of the wolf and the heads of two figures remain.

In the spandrels above are two square panels containing a cockatrice, and another strange beast. The gable is filled with an arcade, the central member of which is corbelled off to make room underneath for three little lancet windows which light the parvise chamber within. The buttresses of the porch have slender shafts at the angles, which are finished off with foliage of a remarkably free and graceful kind; it should be noticed as an example of those subtle touches that are so abundant in this porch. On the buttresses are pinnacles with an arcade, at the top of which little openings cast a shadow that gives a lightness to the whole effect. A smaller pinnacle is at the apex of the gable, and underneath it an ornament of twisted foliage.

Nothing could well surpass the interior of this porch; the delicacy and refinement which are shown in every detail are the more amazing when we consider that the architect and his masons had only just emerged from the large methods of Norman building. A range of three arcades on either side is divided in the midst by three shafts boldly detached from the pear-shaped moulding round which they are grouped. These shafts carry the ribs of the groined vault, and divide the porch into two square bays. Their capitals are very boldly undercut, and bear distinct traces of Romanesque influence; indeed, the volutes of the cap on the west side give it almost the appearance of a very freely-carved Corinthian capital. Those at the angles are of like fashion, except that on the north-east, which has fuller and freer foliage, wherein stands a man shooting with his bow at a bird, the whole most vigorously conceived.

In the uppermost arcade the little touch of foliage that is worked on to the junction of the mullions (which are made up of four pear-shaped mouldings) illustrates the love of delicate things that is so characteristic of this architect. Below is a projecting double arcade, behind which, against the wall, is a

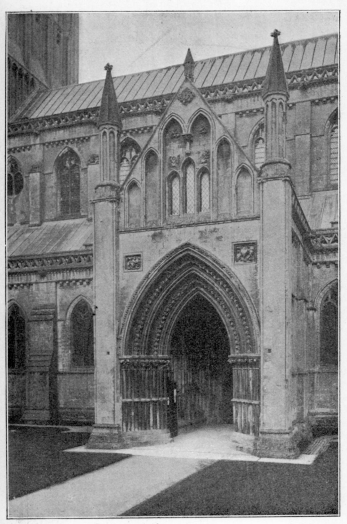

THE NORTH PORCH.

D

third row of arches: the outer mouldings intersect and the abaci of the outer caps are finished off in a carefully restrained curl of foliage; those on the soffit are deeply undercut, by means of which a very black shadow is secured. All the capitals are carved with the stiff-leafed foliage; and in the spandrels are grotesque beasts, full of character. The string-course below is finished with dragons who bend round and swallow the end of the string, their tails (on the west side) twisting right along the moulding. It is significant of the free way in which the masons were employed, that the carving varies very much on the two sides. The grotesques in the spandrels above mentioned are finest on the east side, but the dragons of the string course are best on the west side, where their expressions, as they bite the moulding, are full of life and humour. On this western side, too, the foliage which fills the spandrels of the lowest arcade is at its best; it is indeed the purest and truest piece of decorative work in the whole cathedral. Each moulding in this beautiful porch, from the filleted ribs of the groins to the bands round the shafts, and the moulded edge of the stone bench, is most carefully thought out, and adapted to its position, in a way that every architect will appreciate. The double doorway which leads into the church has an unusual and most effective moulding on its jambs, very large and simple, with slight projections worked upon it: the inner moulding of the enclosing arch, however, is a boldly projecting zig-zag, the supporting capitals of which have two figures, one in a cope, the other a bishop in a very pointed chasuble. The central pillar is of much later date. Above is a square recess filled with later masonry, where perhaps a figure was once inserted.

Most happily, the North Porch has been spared from the restorer's hand. It is a unique and most beautiful example of early work; any restoration of it would practically destroy it, and would be an unpardonable crime. The hungry eye of the modern vandal is sure to seize on this piece of virgin work, sooner or later; for its very purity will tempt him. We only hope that when that day comes the Chapter will be faithful to their trust.

The **gable end** of the north transept, which must be very near to the north porch in date, is a very similar example of the early work. It is flanked by turrets which are capped with pinnacles; both turrets, pinnacles and wall are rich with arcading, the effect of which is especially charming in the gable, where, by a happy device, the weather moulding is made to curve suddenly over the two topmost arches, filling the angle at the apex of the coping, and leaving a little space between it and the two arches to be occupied by foliage.

The general character of the **walls** is distinctly Transitional; the buttresses are almost as low, broad, shallow and massive as in Norman work; and the windows, though now filled with Perpendicular tracery, are so broad that, were they but round-headed, they would look more Norman than much real Norman work.

The richness of exterior effect is much increased by a most graceful Decorated **parapet**, which is carried all round the church on the wall of both nave and aisles.   As for the masonry as a whole, with the exception of the west front nothing could be sounder and more skilfully executed.   Mr Britton's opinion was that " perhaps there is not a church in the kingdom of the same age where the stone has been so well chosen, better put together, and where it remains in so perfect a state : this deserves the particular notice and study of architects." *

The **Chain Gate**, one of the peculiar glories of Wells, is really a bridge over the roadway, built by Bishop Beckington and his executors, to connect the chapter-house staircase with the vicars' close.   Freeman spoke of it as a "marvel of ingenuity," yet perhaps its excellence consists rather in its simplicity.   A covered way was needed to the close, but the road lay between, and so a bridge was built; the bridge had to rest on something : three arches were therefore made, one large for carts, and two small for foot-passengers ; a further space had to be spanned between the road and the staircase : the bridge was therefore continued on the same level, but, as the ground here was lower, the arch on this side was built on a lower level. Furthermore, the two ends of the bridge not being exactly opposite to one another, the bridge had to turn at a slight angle where it reaches the road.   It is just such simple adaptation of means to an end that gave his chance to a medieval architect ; it is this that gives what is called its picturesqueness to an ancient town, it is this that makes

* *Cathedrals*, iv. 98.

nature so picturesque. A modern architect would have
built his bridge in a straight line across the road, and have
pulled down something to avoid the irregularity; he would
not have had the sense of proportion which alone was

Dawkes & Partridge, Photo.]

THE BISHOP'S EYE.

needed to make utility supremely beautiful. The builder
of the Chain Gate just used his opportunities to their very
best. He saw that but a small thing was wanted, that the
close must not be dwarfed; so he kept the work little and
delicate, rich and light: he made its chief beauty to
lie in its *bijou* character. Yet he preserved its dignity by

the wide opening of the central arch, the height of which is emphasised by the smallness of the two arches on either side. But although the two small arches effect so much by their contrast with the large one, the harmony of the gateway is preserved by the panelling above them which marks this part of the bridge off from the rest. On the south of the gate is a blank wall, supported by a buttress which was wanted here, and so here was put. On the south of the buttress is the lower arch which is so admirable a foil both to the height of the main gateway and the delicacy of the windows. A correctly-minded architect would not have tolerated this blank wall and irregularly-placed arch ; but substitute what you will for the wall, or alter the height of the arch, or replace both by an arcade, and the dignity of the little gateway is gone. It may further be noticed that the builder kept the upper and lower stages very distinct, and made the upper storey as clearly a bridge as the lower is a gateway : the charming little windows run in a continuous range over blank wall, gate, and all, but they are grouped closer together over the gate. A battle-mented parapet finishes the top of the bridge. Niches are placed in the midst of the two windows over the gate ; they contain graceful statues of St. Andrew and other saints. In the wide moulding of the string course there are angels, curiously placed in a horizontal position, as well as the stags' heads of Beckington's arms.

Passing under the Chain Bridge a good view of the **chapter-house** is obtained. It is a massive, buttressed octagon, the lower stage marked by the small broad barred windows of the undercroft, the next by the rather squat traceried windows of the house itself, while under the cornice is an open arcade. The gargoyles are interesting. A parapet, different in design and inferior to that of the church itself, finishes the building. From this part of the road, there is a good view of the cathedral in one of its most character-istic aspects ;—the Lady Chapel, the low buildings of the north-eastern transept and retro-choir, the chapter-house in the foreground, all lying on ground below the level of the road, and over the Chain Bridge a glimpse of the north transept gable and the north-west tower.

A queer corner, hidden by a thick tree, is formed between the chapter-house and the choir aisle; in spite of the obscure position, a fine gargoyle of the head and shoulders of a man, carved in unusually colossal proportions, is placed here at a low altitude, to carry off the water that must gather at the junction of aisle with undercroft passage. Through the walls that rise high on either side a capital glimpse of the tower can be had.

From the same road, opposite the prebendal house (now allotted to the Principal of the Theological College), which has a picturesque Perpendicular doorway with a window above, the grouping of the Lady Chapel with the rest of the church can be well seen.

The rich and light appearance of the **east end** is due not only to the charm of its tracery, which contrasts so well with the network of the Lady Chapel windows, and to the parapet which rises slightly in the centre, but also to the three lights which pierce the gable; of these the upper is diamond-shaped, and thus the masonry that is left has the appearance of a stout Y cross.

From the South-East.—One of the most interesting views of the exterior is from the lovely grass-plot on the east of the cloisters, where once stood the cloister Lady Chapel, and where the vicars were formerly buried. It is being again used as a cemetery, which is unfortunate, since there are few things more irreligiously dismal than a modern burial-ground, and already a cluster of marble and granite monuments has arisen to spoil one of the most peaceful and unspoilt places in Wells. If monuments there must be (and why need we so advertise the dead?), let them at least be quiet and humble and beautiful: those ostentatious erections of hard and polished stone ruin the grey walls before which they stand; their frigid materials are too obtrusive for Christian modesty, too enduring for human memory. May we not yet hope that this spot will be spared the fate of the cloister garth?

From here the Lady Chapel is well seen as quite a separate building, joined to the rest of the church only in its lower part, and with its own parapet round all its eight sides; its form harmonises most charmingly with the square presbytery behind it, and with the lofty chapter-house, like itself octagonal. A further beauty is added by the solitary flying buttress which stands out at the south-eastern corner; though certain rents in the southern wall show that the buttress was built for reasons of the gravest utility. On the south side of the chapel there is a little door, covered by what looks at first like a kind of porch, but it is really the passage of a small vestry (p. 132) which was built up against the wall; the roof of the vestry was a little higher than that of the passage, and must have leant against the wall just under the window, as is proved by its gargoyle near the passage door. This vestry was fatuously destroyed in the early part of this century by an official who did not even know that it was medieval work till the soundness of the masonry proved almost too much for his workmen.

The junction between the earlier and the later presbytery is well seen from here—too well seen, in fact, for it is awkwardly managed. The later choir windows, with their crocketed ogee hood-moulds, are a good feature, and so are the flying buttresses; but the high-pitched roof of the earlier aisle is discontinued at the break in order to give room for these windows and buttresses; and the effect of this sudden termination of an aisle roof half-way along a building is not pleasant. In the earlier part, too, the later windows have been clumsily inserted some distance below the Early English dripstone, as if only the internal effect had been considered. The same may also be said of the window in the south transept gable: the gable, by the way, is a much plainer affair than that of the north transept.

Here stood the two **Cloister Lady Chapels,** but unfortunately their sites were not marked on the grass after the excavations were finished three years ago. Thus nothing can be seen from here of the earlier chapel, and, of the later, only the doorway and the Perpendicular panelling against the cloister which marks its western end, and the commencement of the walls. A small quatrefoiled hagioscope may be noticed in the library above the cloister; it, no doubt, commanded a view of the high altar of the chapel.

The earlier *Capella B.M.V. juxta claustrum* is often referred to in the chapter documents, and was a favourite centre of devotion. It became a kind of family chapel for the numerous clan of Byttons, after the first bishop of that name was buried there; it was also sometimes used as a chapter-house. The Early English doorway which led to it can still be seen in the cloister wall, on the right of the present doorway; it is partly covered by an I.H.S. of later date, made with the instruments of the Passion. The excavations of 1894, when the foundations were laid bare under Mr Buckle's direction, showed that this chapel consisted originally of a plain oblong building, earlier even than the north porch in date (*i.e.* before 1185), which was afterwards (c. 1275) enlarged by the addition of an aisle on either side. The excavations showed that arches were used at this time to replace the western part of the older walls, and thus to throw the ancient chapel open to its new aisles. The original chapel, then, if it was not actually part of Bishop Gisa's buildings, spared when John de Villula destroyed Gisa's cloister, seems to have been built not long after Gisa's time, and at least on the site of Gisa's chapel. This would account for its orientation, which was in a more northerly direction than that of the cathedral, and probably was the same as that of the pre-Norman church. Excellent plans of the foundations both of this and the later chapel are to be found in the *Somerset Proceedings* for 1894, where the whole matter is discussed in detail by Canon Church and Mr Edmund Buckle.

The later chapel on this site was built by *Bishop Stillington* (1466-91): it followed the orientation of the cathedral, and was of much larger size than the former building, being about 107 ft. in length. It consisted of a nave, transepts and choir, with fan-tracery vault, of which some fragments have been lately fixed in the cloister wall. Most profusely ornamented and panelled within, as can be seen by the west end against the cloister wall, it is considered to have been the *chef d'œuvre* of the Somerset Perpendicular, surpassing even Sherborne and St. Mary, Redcliffe.

But its glory was not to be for long. Stillington was buried in this "goodly Lady Chapell in the Cloysters," says Godwin, "but rested not long there; for it is reported that divers olde men, who in their youth had not onely seene the celebration of his funeral, but also the building of his tombe, chapell, and all did also see tombe and chapell destroyed, and the bones of the Bishop that built them turned out of the lead in which they were interred." This was in 1552, when Bishop Barlow and the chapter made a grant to that barbarous scoundrel, Sir John Gates, of "the chapple, sett, lyinge and beynge by the cloyster on the south syde of the said Cathedral Church of Wells, commonly called the Ladye Chapple, with all the stones and stonework, ledde, glasse, tymbre, and iron . . . the soyle that the sayd chapple standeth upon only excepted." The condition was that the rubble should be all cleared away, and the ground made "fayre and playn," within four years; but

Dawkes & Partridge, Photo.]
DOORWAY, SOUTH-EAST OF CLOISTER.

before this period had elapsed, Sir John's head had gone the way of the Lady Chapel.

The **Cloister** in its more prominent features is Perpendicular, having been rebuilt in the fifteenth century. Nevertheless the outer walls are of Jocelin's date, together with the doorway leading into the palace (see illustration on this page); and the lower part of the east cloister wall, including the two small

EAST WALK OF CLOISTER.

doorways therein, is said by Mr Buckle to be undoubtedly earlier than Jocelin's time, and contemporary with the north porch, c. 1185. Thus we have still the original plan at least of the thirteenth-century cloisters. This plan is characteristic of a non-monastic church, where the cloister is not the centre of a common life, but merely an ornamental convenience which might or might not be added, and when added might be of any fashion that was desired. There is no walk on the north side, no refectory or dormitory, and the plan is not square, as would be the case with a conventual building, but an irregular parallelogram, while the eastern walk is built up against the south end of the transept instead of against its western wall.

The inner part of Jocelin's cloister was probably a wooden penthouse like that of Glastonbury. At all events, it has entirely disappeared. The eastern alley was built by the executors of Bishop Bubwith, who died in 1424. That on the west, with its rooms, was built by Beckington (1443-65) and his executors. That on the south was completed soon after by Thomas Henry, the treasurer. Beckington, by the way, showed a reckless disregard of the earlier work by carrying his cloister right up against the south-west tower, and completely concealing the beautiful arcading of that part. Beckington's executors, in the time of Bishop Stillington, also built the singing school over the western cloister. Bubwith's executors built the northern part of the library over the eastern cloister; but the southern part was added at a later date. The square windows were inserted later still by the famous Dr Busby, about 1670. The fourteen bays of lierned vaulting over the east alley, and one on the south, were executed in 1457-8 by John Turpyn Lathamo, at the cost, we find from the fabric roll, of ¾d. per foot, or £6, 11s. 3d. for the whole, though an additional ten shillings was presented to him for his diligence.

Each alley consists of thirteen bays in the Perpendicular style; the windows are now all unglazed, of six lights, with transoms and tracery; between the windows are buttresses to support the rooms above, which extend, however, only over the east and west alleys. Turpyn's vaulting is of a curiously decadent character, which reminds one of the Jacobean Gothic of Oxford and Cambridge. The ribs spread at the start to enclose a trefoiled panel, and they curve into one another when they meet at the bosses. In the rest of the south walk, however, the bosses are square, and receive the ribs in the usual manner; in the west walk they are still square, and more varied in their ornament, bearing Beckington's initials, arms, and rebus, arranged in several different ways. Beckington's arms, which occur also on the gateways, are argent on a fess azure, between in chief three bucks' heads caboshed gules, and in base as many pheons sable, a bishop's mitre or. His rebus is a fire *beacon* lighted, a *tun* holding the fire.

Two small stone pent-houses, of which the purpose is uncertain, are built up against the windows of the fourth and sixth bays of the eastern alley. The vault of this alley was built without reference to the fine Early English doorway into the transept, one side of which it hides, the weather moulding being cut away. This doorway is mentioned in an Act of the Chapter of 1297, but it was probably made by Jocelin before he built the cloister wall, which comes uncomfortably near to the door, as if it were an afterthought. The companion doorway from the western alley, which was the usual entrance to the cathedral in the thirteenth century, has been similarly defaced by the vault. Three annual fairs used to be held in the cemetery, till Bishop Reginald set apart for the purpose the new ground which is still the market-place. The traditional entrance to the church by this south-western porch may have been due to the fact that the citizens gathered for secular business on the south-western side. At the south end of the eastern alley is the Early English bishop's doorway, which no doubt led straight to the palace in the days when there was no moat to obstruct this route. The door was originally hung to open inwards; a beautiful moulding was destroyed to hang it in its present position. There is a bracket of later date over this doorway.

The cloister-garth, which is hideous with modern tombstones, is traditionally called the *Palm Churchyard*, no doubt because of the yew which grows there. Yew trees, so common in churchyards, are still commonly called palms, because their branches were used for the procession on Palm Sunday. This churchyard was anciently the burial-place of the canons, the ground east of the cloister (now used again as a cemetery) being reserved for the vicars, while the space before the west front was the lay burial-ground.

An admirably contrived *dipping-place* was still standing in the Palm churchyard, near the second bay of the east cloister, within the memory of living persons, but now no trace of it remains above ground. A water-course, held within a channel of carefully-worked masonry, runs under the eastern cloister from St. Andrew's well, and passes on to fall ultimately into the old mill-stream. The oblong building over it that formed the dipping-place was entered at the south end, and a few steps (with aumbries for the linen at either side) led to the washing-place at the little stream. An arch covered this spot, where the water ran through two low arches on either side and was bridged in the midst by a pavement. The place was used for washing linen, and the water required for the cathedral was drawn here before the modern supply pipes were introduced.

The Library is over the east walk of the cloister, and is entered from the south transept. It is a charming old-world place, full of ancient volumes, many of which are of great interest. A passage runs from end to end, along the east side of the long room, the other side being mainly occupied by the old desks, benches and bookcases, which project at right angles to the wall, many of the book-chains still hanging on them. There are said to be over three thousand volumes, including the bulk of Bishop Ken's library, a collection of early editions of his works, and his copy of Bishop Andrewe's "Devotions." There are also several books (including one Aldine "Aristotle") with MS. notes and autograph of Erasmus. The collection of old charters, which have recently been made to throw so much light on the history of the cathedral, is also preserved here. Some of the most interesting charters are displayed in glass cases ; one of them, Edgar's grant to Ealhstane, is specially venerable for the signature of St. Dunstan—*Ego Dunstan Ep.*—which occurs third among the witnesses to the document.

Two precious relics of medieval times are also kept here. One, which is generally called a lantern, was till lately hung in the undercroft. There is no trace of its ever having been used as a lantern, and it is probably the wooden *canopy of the pyx* which hung before the high altar. The Blessed Sacrament was in medieval times reserved, not in a tabernacle, but in a hanging pyx of precious metal; and this graceful wooden canopy probably contained the pyx. There are only two other possible examples of the pyx-canopy (at

Milton Abbas and Tewkesbury), and both are of later date than this, which is thirteenth century. Woodwork of this period is so rare that, even were it not a pyx-canopy, it would be of extreme interest. It is cylindrical in form, divided into three storeys of open tracery, and crowned with a cresting of three-lobed leaves. Its height is 3 ft. $11\frac{1}{4}$ in., its internal diameter $14\frac{1}{2}$ inches. It is made of oak, certain parts of a later restoration being of deal. Mr St. John Hope (*Proc. of Soc. of Antiquaries*, 1897), thus enumerates the traces of colour : "The whole of the body and its upper and lower rings have been painted red, with gold flowers or other devices upon the transverse bands. The slender dividing shafts seem to have been coloured blue. The leaves of the cresting have apparently been painted white, but the circular boss in the middle of each leaf was entirely red." Two pairs of iron rods, with a ring and swivel hook, serve to suspend it in a steady position.

The other relic is the thirteenth-century *crozier* which was recently found in a tomb in the cathedral, and probably belongs to the time of Savaric, though there is no evidence, beyond its style, for describing it as his crozier. It was dug up in a stone coffin in the western burial-ground of the cathedral in the time of Dean Lukin (1799-1812). It is thus described in the *Catalogue* of the Burlington Fine Arts Club exhibition of enamels, June 1897 : "A complete crozier, [the staff] wooden (modern), with enamelled head one foot in length. Limoges, thirteenth century. The volute is a serpent with blue scales and serrated crest, enclosing a winged figure of St. Michael and a dragon studded with turquoises. The knop is encased in pierced repoussé open work formed of dragons, and the socket ornamented with thirteenth-century foliated scrolls in these slightly spiral bands, separated by jewelled dragons whose tails form three rings under the knop." St. Michael is represented in the act of attacking the dragon with his spear.

A little **Museum** has been formed in one of the rooms over the western cloister. It contains a collection of seals, Mr Buckle's plans of the cloisters and the Cloister Lady Chapel excavations, and many other objects of interest.

The principal buildings in connection with the cathedral are the vicars' close, the bishop's palace, the deanery, the archdeaconry, and the canons' houses. There are also Beckington's fine gates,—the Chain Gate by the vicars' close,

THE CHAIN GATE, ENTRANCE TO CLOSE, 1824.

Brown's, or the Dean's Gate, near the deanery; the Penniless Porch, leading from the Market Place to the cathedral;

E

and the Bishop's Eye, leading from the Market Place to the palace.

Most deservedly famous is the unrivalled **Vicars' Close**, which contains the houses built by Bishop Ralph and his successors for the vicars-choral.   Passing through the gate, one sees the two long ranges of quiet and lovely houses, fronted by their little gardens, with a roadway betwixt them. Nothing can surpass this arrangement for its peaceful seclusion and constant charm, not even the square quadrangles and cloisters of Oxford, and yet, so convenient is it, that no better model could be chosen should there ever come any general return to the old collegiate life ; for a settlement, for a model factory, one can imagine nothing better even now.   There are forty-two houses, twenty-one on either side : each con-sisted originally of two rooms, one above the other, with a staircase ; for the vicars were single men.   Now that the vicars-choral are married, many of them live in the town, but all the theological students are lodged here, and there are always a few rooms to be let to those visitors who are wise enough to stay in this charming place.

The tall chimneys rise up through the eaves of the little houses ; octagonal at the top, they are perforated like a lantern, with two openings on each side.   On them are shields bearing the arms of the see, of Bishop Beckington and his executors, Swan, Sugar, and Pope, sugar-loaves and swans abounding in the decoration.

At the farther end of the close is the tiny chapel (finished by Bubwith, and finally consecrated in 1489, after Beckington had added the wooden ceiling and the chamber above), where compline is still said by the theological students.   It is one of the most beautiful things in Wells—a jewel, like so much of its period—and it has been well decorated in sgraffitto and colour by Mr Heywood Sumner.   An interesting feature of its exterior is that some of the old Early English carving was worked in with the masonry of the wall, by way of decoration, and very effective it is.   A passage at the side leads to the Liberty, where are some of the prebendal houses.

Over the entrance, and leading into the bridge of the Chain Gate, are the hall and its offices, which are approached by a fine staircase.   In the hall is a painting of much interest, which represents Bishop Ralph seated on his throne, the vicars kneeling before him; the petition which he holds runs—*Per vicos positi villae, Pater alme rogamus, Ut simul uniti, te, Dante domos maneamus;* and the answer, which has the episcopal seal, is—*Vestra petunt merita, Quod sint concessu petita: Ut maneatis ita, Loca fecimus hic stabilita.* On the right are seventeen figures with ruffles, evidently added in Elizabethan times; corresponding inscription has also been added—*Quas primus struxit,* etc.

There is also a pulpit over the fireplace, which is large, with good mouldings and an inscription, *In vestris preci habeat* *comedatu dom Ricardu Pomroy quem salvet Ihs. Amen.* On the hearth are a pair of fine fire-dogs.

Just outside the entrance to the vicars' close is a beautiful **oriel window**, which has been much copied in modern times. It springs from a corbelled head, from which foliate four cinquefoiled panels. The window now has only three square-headed lights, the centre one being large. Under its sills are rich panels, and it is capped by a slight crenelated cornice with a boldly-carved drip, from which springs a conical roof surmounted by a fleur-de-lys.

The beautiful **Bishop's Palace** was mainly built by Jocelin, who died in 1242. It consists of three sides of a quadrangle, the bishop's house being on the east, the chapel on the south, the kitchen and offices running alongside the moat on the north: on the west side there was formerly a gate-tower and a wall having a cloister within which led to chapel and hall. In addition to these buildings the great hall, now in ruins—forming, with the walls and outhouses, an outer court—was built to the south-west of the chapel. The whole group of buildings stands on a piece of ground, rich with trees, surrounded by a lovely old wall and moat, the single approach being by the bridge and the gate-house, which has Renaissance windows and retains the slit for the portcullis and the drawbridge-chains. Bishop Ralph of Shrewsbury constructed the gate-house and fortifications, which form an irregular pentagon, with a bastion at each angle, and an extra one in the south-east side. The bastion in the western angle (on the south of the gate-house) contains two storeys, of which the lower, called the cow-house or stock-house, was used as a prison for criminous clerks. The moat is fed by a stream from St. Andrew's well hard by.

The palace itself is a most interesting example of medieval architecture, and remains very much in its original condition. It is oblong in plan, and divided lengthwise by a solid wall, running through both storeys from end to end, at about one third of its width; the long outer chamber formed by this wall on the ground floor is divided into the entrance hall of three bays (containing a fireplace, *temp.* Henry VIII.), and the passages to staircase and to chapel at either end. The wider chamber within the wall is lighted by plain lancet windows,

Dawkes & Partridge, Photo.]

THE BISHOP'S PALACE.

and has a row of slender Purbeck pillars down the middle, which, with the corbels on the wall, carry a groined vault: this, the "crypt," or undercroft, was probably used as a storage-room; it is now the dining-room. To the north of this hall is a square chamber with a pillar in the centre; and to the east of the chamber a small room projects beyond the ground plan of the building, with a space at one end (probably a closet) now walled up.

On the first floor the great chamber (68 by 28 feet) stood over the undercroft, while on its north was the bishop's private room, both open to the roof, and to the east of this, his private chapel. The gallery above the entrance hall was formerly divided into three chambers, the two larger of which Mr Buckle thinks were used as a lobby and a wardrobe. The windows in the gallery were restored by Mr Ferrey in 1846, but nothing is new except the marble shafts and bases. The two windows at the north end of the great chamber are evidently later additions, as they have fully developed bar-tracery, while the other windows in the chamber consist of pairs of trefoil-headed windows with a quatrefoil in plate tracery above them

The **Great Hall**, which is now but a beautiful ruin, was built by Bishop Burnell, who died 1292. It was a magnificent chamber, 115 feet by 59½, with high traceried windows. It was divided into nave and aisles by rows of pillars to carry the roof and the passage at the west end led between buttery and pantry to the kitchen; over these rooms was a large solar, and on the north side a porch with staircase at the side leading to the solar. Both hall and palace are well and fully described by Mr Buckle in the *Somerset Proceedings* for 1888. Bishop Barlow had the hall dismantled, employing Sir John Gates for the purpose; the walls, however, were left standing until Bishop Law's time, when they were partly demolished in order to make the ruin more "picturesque."

The chapel is very similar in style to the hall, and was built very shortly afterwards; it is at present defaced by bad decoration and fittings. The carving is very fine and varied; some of the capitals retain the old stiff-leaf foliage, while in some the leaves grow freely round the bell in the Decorated manner. The vaulted ceiling is also an excellent example of the transitional work of the period. The west window is of later date, and has been twice restored—once by Bishop Montague (1608-16), and again in the present century. On the north side, at some height from the ground, are the indications of what may have been a gallery used as a private pew.

Bishop Beckington (1443-66) added the northern block of buildings, now considerably altered, the kitchen and various offices, *le botrye, cellarium, le bakehous, ad lez stues ad nutriendos pisces*, in William of Worcester's words, as well as the gate now called the Bishop's Eye, *aliam portam ad introitum de le palays*, and the parlour (*parluram*) and guest-chambers adjoining the kitchen. This block lies very prettily alongside the moat.

Unfortunately the palace, which had so wonderfully escaped the brutal adaptations of the eighteenth-century architect, was restored in 1846 by Mr Ferrey, and its west front completely altered. The upper storey, the porch, the buttresses were all added by Mr Ferrey; not to mention the tower at the north and the turret at the south, and the conservatory. Bishop Bagot, at whose order the work was done, also rebuilt the kitchen and offices; in fact, he did what he could to destroy the unique character and beauty of a block of buildings without parallel anywhere.

The Bishop's Barn, which stands in a field near the palace is remarkable for its length (110 ft. by 25½) and the number of its buttresses. Simple in character, stately in proportions, it is a striking instance of the perfect sense of fitness which marked the medieval builders : in fact, it is the exact opposite to what a modern builder would erect if asked to provide a barn in the Gothic style.

The Deanery, rebuilt by Dean Gunthorpe (1472-98), is an almost perfect specimen of a fifteenth-century house, in spite of the modern sash windows and other alterations which deface it. As at the palace, the principal apartments were on the first floor; and of these the chief is the hall, an excellent example of the more comfortable late medieval arrangement. Two handsome oriel windows with vaults of fan-tracery are at the upper end, not quite opposite to each other, where the sideboards used to stand ; and at the lower end a stone arch carries a small music-gallery, with three small windows opening to the hall. Under this arch is the lavatory, a stone niche, in which a small cistern was suspended, with a drain at the bottom ; so that the diners could put their hands under the tap of the little cistern as they passed into dinner.

Over the hall are guest chambers with fine windows; and behind the partition at the back of the dais is another chamber with a large window, which Mr J. H. Parker thought to have been the chapel.

Fuller description of the various ecclesiastical buildings can be found in Mr Parker's paper in the *Somerset Proceedings* for 1863.

The Archdeaconry was built in the time of Edward I., but the front of the house has been entirely modernised. The hall is larger than that of the deanery, and occupies the whole height of the building, having a very fine early fifteenth-century open timber roof.

The Choirmaster's House, at the east end of the cathedral, is a fairly perfect example of a fifteenth-century house, retaining its beautiful porch unspoiled. The roof and upper part of the windows of the hall remain, but are disguised and concealed by modern partitions. It is now the residence of the Principal of the Theological College.

An organist's house once communicated with the singing-school, which is over the western cloister; it was much defaced in the eighteenth century, and entirely removed a few years ago.

The Canons' Houses, which lie in the Liberty to the north of the cathedral, have been either entirely rebuilt, or much spoilt by alterations.

The Schoolhouse is partly of the fourteenth century, with wings added in the fifteenth and sixteenth centuries; it retains some features of interest.

Bishop Bubwith's Almshouse is near St. Cuthbert's Church. It was much spoilt in the fifties: the original plan was a great hall, with a chapel at the end of it, and cells along the side for the almsmen. These cells were open at the top so that there was plenty of fresh air, and if an almsman became ill or infirm, he could hear the service chanted daily in the chapel without leaving his bed. At the west end of the hall is a building of two storeys built by the bishop's executors, given to the citizens of Wells as a Guildhall, and used for that purpose till about 1779. Here is preserved a very fine money chest of the fifteenth century, painted with a scroll pattern, and resting on a stand inscribed with curious doggerel of the date 1615.

St. Cuthbert's Church, which, to the scandal of Wells, is kept continually shut, is thus described by Mr J. H. Parker in the *Builder* for 1862 (p. 655):—

"It was originally a cruciform church of the thirteenth century with a central tower, and with aisles to the nave; but of the church all that remains in the original state is a part of the north aisle. The central tower has been removed, the church entirely rebuilt in the fifteenth century. The pillars and arches of the nave have been rebuilt in the fifteenth century also, and the pillars lengthened considerably. The arches, with their dripstones, preserved and used again on the taller pillars, and most of the capitals have had the foliage cut off. The aisle walls, the clerestory, and roof, are all Late Perpendicular, about the time of Henry VII.; but the beautiful west tower is evidently earlier than the clerestory and roof, and has the mark of the old roof on the east side of it, coming below the present clerestory. This fine tower, which is certainly one of the finest of its class, and which Mr Freeman considers, I believe, to rank only second to one other [Wrington], is said to have been built in the time of Bishop Bubwith, or about 1430; and this appears to me probable. The character of the work is rather Early Perpendicular, and the groined vault under the belfry appears to be an imitation of the Decorated vault of the cathedral."

CHAPTER III

THE INTERIOR

THE earlier architecture of Wells Cathedral presents so many puzzles, that the most skilled experts have differed widely both from each other, and, as we know now, from the truth. There are four distinct varieties of Early English work, covering a period of about a century from the time of Bishop Reginald, whose episcopate began in 1174; and yet, until Mr Bennett deciphered the old charters, which have at length settled the problem, all the work was attributed to Jocelin, for nothing was known of Reginald's building, and some of the best judges were even convinced that the west front was built before the nave. The difficulty was mainly caused by the unusual character of the architecture of the nave; "unlike that of any ordinary English building, and belonging to a style on the whole fifty years earlier" than the west front, as Professor Willis said, who gave it a name of its own, and called it the Somerset style. Thus the theory came to be that two bodies of masons had been employed—an ordinary English company for the front, and a local Somerset company for the nave, transepts and choir, who worked in a local variation of the prevalent Early English style. In this way, an attempt was made to overcome the difficulty of attributing to Jocelin work which Mr Willis had himself pronounced to be "only a little removed from the early Norman style." Mr Freeman, too, had allowed that the north porch might be earlier than Jocelin; and, long before, Britton had said that there would be little hesitation in ascribing the church to the transitional period of Henry II. (1154-89) on architectural evidence, were it not for Godwin's assertion, that Jocelin had entirely pulled down the old church and built a fresh one.

But now we have got behind Godwin, and have found from contemporary evidence that Bishop Reginald commenced the present church. Thus we are able to divide the Early English work into no less than four periods. (1) The three western arches of the choir, with the four western bays of its aisles, the transepts, and the four eastern bays of the nave, which are Reginald's work (1174-1191), and so early as to be still in a state of transition from the Norman. It is a unique example of transitional building, and Willis calls it "an improved Norman, worked with considerable lightness and richness, but distinguished from the Early English by greater massiveness and severity." The characteristics of this late twelfth-century work are bold round mouldings, square abaci, capitals, some with traces of the classical volute, others interwoven with fanciful imagery that reminds us of the Norman work of Glastonbury ; while in the north porch, which must be the earliest of all, we even find the zig-zag Norman moulding. (2) The rest of the nave, which was finished in Jocelin's time—that is to say, in the first half of the thirteenth century—preserves the main characteristics of the earlier work, though the flowing sculptured foliage becomes more naturalistic, and lacks the quaint intermingling of figure subjects. (3) The west front, which is Jocelin's work, and alone can claim to be of pure Early English style. (4) The chapter-house crypt, which is so late as to be almost Transitional, though, curiously enough, it contains the characteristic Early English dog-tooth moulding which is found nowhere else except in the west window. From this, we reach the Early Decorated of the staircase, the full Decorated of the chapter-house itself, the later Decorated of the Lady Chapel, the transitional Decorated of the presbytery, and the full Perpendicular of the western towers.

Much of the masonry in the transepts, choir, choir aisles, and even in the eastern transepts, bears the peculiar diagonal lines which are the marks of Norman tooling. This does not, of course, prove that any part of Bishop Robert's church is standing, for medieval builders were notoriously economical in using up old masonry, but it does show that there are more remains of his work in the building than was generally supposed. A characteristic feature in this Norman tooling is that if a rule be laid along its lines, they will be found to be very slightly curved, a feature which is due to the fact that Norman masons dressed their stones with the broad curved blade of an axe.

THE NAVE.

The plan of the church is remarkably complete, symmetrical, and well-proportioned. Nave, transepts, choir, each flanked with its aisles, combine to form with the Lady Chapel and chapter-house a cathedral church which, though not of the first magnitude, is the most complete and typical in England. The ground plan itself, as set out in all technical severity on page 160, possesses an unusual attraction for the eye. It is free both from multilation and excrescences; and yet all the picturesque external grouping, and internal mystery, which the afterthoughts of Gothic architects so often lend to a building, are secured, in the case of Wells, by the carefully-placed chapter-house and the beautiful arrangement of the Lady Chapel. The transepts of the choir are very happily carried far enough east to be internally subordinate to this chapel, which arrangement, with the apsidal form of the chapel itself, adds much to the beautiful proportions of the church. A third transept is given to the west end of the nave by the two towers.

The length of Wells Cathedral from east to west is 383 feet within the walls, and 415 without. The length of the nave is 192 feet, its breadth 82 feet, and its height 67 feet. The length of the choir is 117 feet, and its height 73 feet. The transepts are 131 feet within and 150 feet without.

The Nave.—The general effect of the nave is that of length rather than height, and this is mainly due to the continuous arcade of the triforium which leads the eye from end to end of the building instead of from floor to roof. If this be compared with the older work in the transepts, it will be seen at once by how simple a device this radical change in the effect has been produced. Instead of being carried down right across the triforium, as in the transepts, the triple vaulting shafts are cut off above the arcade so as to be little more than corbels, and the space thus gained is used to give one additional opening to each bay of the triforium. In the transepts the triforium is composed of pairs of lancet arches separated by vaulting shafts, the triforium of each bay being a distinct composition over its pier arch; but by the time the architect had come to the nave, a new idea had occurred to him, and he made the triforium in one continuous arcade, unbroken from east to west, evidently with the deliberate intention of producing a horizontal rather than a vertical effect. The arrangement has undoubtedly a character of its own, and "there is no nave in which the eye is so irresistibly carried eastward as in that of Wells."

In spite of this method of securing an effect of length, the builders managed to make the most of the small height of their church. The manner in which this was done forms an interesting example of the subtle feeling of proportion which early architects possessed. The clerestory was made unusually lofty, and the comparative lowness of the triforium both adds to the soaring effect and prevents the horizontal appearance being overmastering. This is increased by the bold vaulting of the ceiling, and the way in which the lantern arches fit into the vault.

But, homogeneous as the nave appears, a little examination will clearly reveal the break which marks the separation between the late twelfth-century work of Reginald de Bohun and the thirteenth-century continuation of Jocelin. The earlier work, as we have seen, consisted of the four eastern bays, which, with the present ritual choir and transepts, formed Reginald's church; and, as a matter of fact, at the fifth bay (the next bay westward of the north porch) the marks of change are so evident that all writers upon the cathedral have based their theories upon it. The earlier masonry in the spandrels on the east of this point consists of small stones indifferently set: the later masonry is made up of larger blocks more carefully laid together; in the earlier part there are small heads at the angles of the pier arches, in the later there are none, while the small heads in the angles of the earlier triforium arcade give place to larger heads in the later; the tympana, which fill the heads of the lancets in this arcade, also are mainly ornamented in the earlier part with grotesque beasts, while in the later they contain foliage, with two exceptions. Again, the medallions which decorate the spaces above the triforium are sunk in the earlier masonry, but, in the later, they are flush with the surface and not so deeply carved. Even more noticeable is the difference in the capitals, those of the western bays being lighter, freer, and more under-cut, though less interesting and hardly as beautiful as those of the earlier part. With the exception of these differences, however, which are doubtless due to the freedom enjoyed by medieval workmen, the original design of the nave was faithfully adhered to, the square abaci, even, being retained, though the circular abacus had become a leading characteristic of the true Early English of Jocelin's period. Certainly it is an unusual instance of an architect deliberately setting himself to complete the works of an earlier period in faithful accordance with the original plan; and we may well be grateful to him for his modesty.

All the carving is most interesting and beautiful: the caps and corbels of the vaulting - shafts; the little heads at the

T. W. Phillips, Photo.]
A CAPITAL—THE FRUIT-STEALER'S PUNISHMENT.

angles of the arches, which are vivid sketches of every type of contemporary character; and the carvings in the tympana, above referred to, which are best in the seventh, eighth, and ninth bays (counting from the west end), those on the north excelling in design and execution, while those on the south are more grotesque. But the **capitals** of the piers are the best of all, and the most hurried visitor should spare some time for the study of these remarkable specimens of sculpture, vigorous and life-like, yet always subordinated to their architectural purpose. Those in the transepts are perhaps the best (p. 89), but the following in the nave should not be missed :—

North Side, sixth Pier.—(By north porch) Birds pluming their wings : Beast licking himself : Ram : Bird with human head, holding knife (?).

Eighth Pier.—Fox stealing goose, peasant following with stick : Birds pruning their feathers : (Within Bubwith's chapel) Human monster with fish's tail, holding a fish : Bird holding frog in his beak, which is extremely long and delicate.

Ninth Pier.—Pedlar carrying his pack on his shoulders, a string of large beads in one hand.

Toothless monster, with hands on knees.

South side, seventh Pier.—Birds with human heads, one wearing a mitre.

Eighth Pier.—Peasant, with club, seized by a lion : Bird with curious foliated tail : (Within St. Edmund's chapel) Owl : Peasant with mallet (?).

The lofty clerestory windows are divided into two lights by Perpendicular tracery of late fourteenth or early fifteenth century date, which extends to the level of the passage, the lower part being filled with masonry. The windows were not, however, altered in shape when the tracery was inserted. In the tracery are very slight traces of the old glass.

The triforium passage is capacious enough to form a large tunnel, which gives a good effect to its lancet openings. The small iron rings, which are prominent enough to be rather tiresome to the eye, were recently inserted for the use of those engaged in cleaning the walls. Within the passage additional arches may be seen, inserted to strengthen the arcade at the commencement of the later work and in other places.

The groined ceiling has carved bosses at the intersection of its ribs. The red pattern is a restoration of the old design which was found on the removal of the whitewash, but the restorer seems to have missed the right tints.

There is a music-gallery in the clerestory of the sixth bay on the south side ; it is composed of three panels with quatrefoils containing plain shields, and is finished with an embattled cornice. Another gallery, perhaps for an organ, must have been supported by the two noticeable brackets on the spandrels of the fourth bay of the same side. One may conjecture that it was of wood, and was reached from the triforium. The brackets are carved in the shape of very large heads of a bishop and a king, both supported by smaller heads, and of an extremely benevolent expression. The hair of the king has that curious formal twist with which we are familiar on playing-cards. As some of the small heads in the chapter-house have the same style of hair, these two brackets probably belong to the end of the thirteenth century.

Sir John Harrington in the *Nugae Antiquae* (ii. 148) says of these two heads that "the old men of Wells had a tradi-

T. W. Phillips, Photo.]

A CAPITAL—TOOTHACHE.

tion, that, when there should be such a king and such a bishop, then the church should be in danger of ruin." At the time of the Reformation it was noticed that the head of the king bore a certain resemblance to Henry VIII., and that the king held in his hands a child falling, who, it was said, could be none other than Edward VI. The peculiarity of the bishop's figure is that he has women and children about him. "This fruitful bishop, they affirmed, was Dr Barlow (p. 156), the first married bishop of Wells, and perhaps of England. This talk being rife in Wells in Queen Mary's time, made him rather affect Chichester at his return than Wells, where not only the things that were ruined but those that remained, served for records and remembrances of his sacrilege."

The west end of the nave is covered in its lower portion by an arcade of five arches with Purbeck shafts, the middle one being wider than the rest, to contain the two smaller arches of the doorway. The three lancet windows were re-modelled in Perpendicular times by the insertion of the triple shafts, which have the casement mouldings and angular caps of the period ; but the dog-tooth moulding of the arches, the medallions in the spandrels, and the little corbel heads of the Early English work remain. A Perpendicular parapet along the sill of the window marks the gallery which, pierced through the splays, carries the triforium passage round the end of the

SPECIMENS OF CAPITALS.

nave. A string course runs along the bottom of this gallery and forms the bases of the triple shafts ; the bases are supported on corbels which die off upon the sloping wall below. This wall conceals a curious gallery, the purpose of which is not known ; it is entered by steps from the triforium, and lighted by round openings which can be seen in the central quatrefoils of the west front ; when these quatrefoils were filled with sculpture it would have been difficult to detect the existence of the dark gallery.

Two small transepts at the west end of the nave are formed by the western towers, which project in this church beyond the aisles. These transepts are connected with the aisles by an arch, the lower part of which is closed by wooden doors. That on the north was used as a chapel of the Holy Cross, and of late years as the consistory court: it is now the choir-boys' vestry; that on the south served as a porch in the days when the usual entrance to the church was by the Early English doorway which leads into it from the cloister; it is now appropriated to the bell-ringers. They are both of strikingly different style to the rest of the interior, as they were built in pure Early English style, at the same time as the west front, of which the towers form, of course, an integral part. Their shafts are of blue lias, the capitals richly carved; their groined vaults have a circular opening to admit to the upper storey of the tower, which has its corbels ornamented

A CAPITAL.

with foliage, although they cannot be seen. Over the doorway in the south chapel an arcade is curiously fitted into the available space beneath the vault.

The Aisles of the Nave (see p. 19) are of the same character as the nave itself, the later part having been resumed at about the same time, and at the same place. Among the capitals the following in the north aisle may be specially mentioned:—

Fifth Shaft.—Peasants carrying sheep, etc., a dog in the midst.

Ninth Shaft.—Man in rough coat, which falls before and behind rather like a chasuble, carrying foliage on his back. A very good figure.

Tenth Shaft.—(By arch of vestry) Man carrying what seems to be a hod of mortar and a mason's mallet.

Opposite side of arch, at end of the string course : Peasant in hood carrying a staff. On the caps opposite are two heads with tongues on their teeth (see p. 92).

The windows, both of these aisles and those of the transepts, were filled with Perpendicular tracery at about the same time as the clerestory windows. The date of this addition must have been before Bishop's Bubwith's time, for the library which that prelate built over the cloister blocks the south window of the west aisle of the south transept. A stone bench runs along all the aisles.

Glass of the Nave, Transepts, and Aisles.—Most of the glass of the west window was collected abroad, during his

SPECIMENS OF CAPITALS.

exile, by Bishop Creyghton, while he was yet dean (1660-70). The main part of it is devoted to the life and death of St. John Baptist, and is of excellent early sixteenth-century work, for under the fantastic figure of the executioner is the inscription *Sancti Johannis Decollatio* 1507. The two other lights containing the large figures of King Ina and Bishop Ralph are, however, of later date, and to judge by their costume they should belong to Creyghton's own time ; moreover, on the southern one are Creyghton's arms. Apparently the compositions at the extreme top and bottom of the middle light are much later ; a little handbook on the cathedral by Mr John Davies, the verger in 1814, states that the then dean and chapter re-arranged and restored the window in 1813 ; these additions must belong to that time, and according to him they were brought from Rouen. Their ugly reds and blues certainly do not blend with the earlier glass, as do the figures of Ina and Ralph, but considerably mar the mellow and delicate

Dawkes & Partridge, Photo.]
VIEW ACROSS NAVE, SHEWING SUGAR'S AND
BUBWITH'S CHAPELS.

effect of the whole. There are only a few slight fragments of old glass in the other windows. There are also two modern windows at the west end of the aisles.

Bishop Bubwith's Chantry Chapel.—Two chantry

chapels stand opposite each other under the ninth pier-arches of the nave. They are alike in general characteristics, though there is an interval of sixty years between them. The chantry of Bishop Bubwith (*ob.* 1424), who built the north-west tower, is formed by a hexagonal screen between the piers, the three eastern sides being filled with a reredos that gives the chapel a square appearance within. The screen is composed of the most light and elaborate tracery, its corners surmounted by a crest; it is open above, but has a rather coarsely-carved canopy over where the altar stood. Doorways, whose jambs are too delicately carved to have ever carried doors, give free access and a clear view of the interior from either side. Altogether it was an ideal place for votive Celebrations, when but few worshippers were present. The niches over the altar have been hacked level with the wall, and the little pillar piscina is also defaced. The triple shafts of the pier at the western end are corbelled off, the corbel being carved with Bubwith's arms (argent, a fess engrailed sable between twelve holly leaves vert, 4, 4, 4, and 4, arranged in quadrangles) impaled with those of the see. The altar here was formerly dedicated to St. Saviour.

Sugar's Chantry.—In the ninth bay of the nave, on the south side, is the chantry of Treasurer Hugh Sugar. Before its erection, the altar of St. Edmund of Canterbury, who was canonised in 1246, stood here; and perhaps, when it comes to be used again, it will be maintained in honour of that most attractive scholar saint. Speaking of these chantries, which were endowed in such profusion in the later Middle Ages, Canon Church (*Somerset Proceedings*, 1888, ii. 103) says: "The belief in the communion of saints, living and dead, and the desire for continued remembrance after death, and for the intercessions of the living, led practically to the endowment of chantries and obits, whereby not only was the church enriched, and the services of many priests provided for, but also attachment to the church of their fathers was greatly strengthened, as being the common home of the dead and the living." That attachment, one would think, is hardly likely to be revived by this beautiful chapel and its fellow being put to base uses. At present it serves as a kind of booking-office, where visitors deposit their sixpences and sign their names, while the other is stored with hassocks, and becomes the resting-place of any brooms, pails, and dustpans that are in use.

St. Edmund's (or Sugar's) chapel is hexagonal, like that of Bishop Bubwith, but its tracery, frieze, and reredos are more elaborate. The canopy over the altar is vaulted with lace-like fan-tracery. Five niches, now empty of their figures, form the reredos ; their sumptuous pedestals and canopies are in excellent condition. Attached to the frieze without, on either side, are six demi-angels, with delicate wings and extremely curly hair, bearing shields, with representations of the Five Wounds, the Lily of the Annunciation, between angels' wings ; the arms of the see (a plain saltire surmounting a pastoral staff in pale between two keys addorsed, the bows interlaced on the dexter, and a sword erect on the sinister) ; the arms of Glastonbury Abbey (a cross flory, in dexter chief a demi-virgin with child proper), the arms of the vicars (a saltire), the initials H. S., and Sugar's arms, originally a "canting coat," three sugar-loaves, and in chief a doctor's cap. Sugar's initials and arms also occur under the canopy. It is the fashion to consider this chapel inferior to its fellow, merely because it is later in date, but a little impartial study will show that it is much the better of the two. The tracery, though less uncommon, is more graceful, that over the doorway especially being far better contrived ; the cornice is better proportioned, and is not spoilt by the untidy trail of foliage which runs round that of Bubwith's chapel ; the canopy, too, fits in with the curve of the tracery, while that of the others projects clumsily across it.

The Pulpit.—From the west end of this chapel steps lead into the stone pulpit which adjoins it. This pulpit was built in Henry VIII.'s reign, by Bishop Knight, who died in 1547. It is a low, but well-proportioned, structure, resting on a basement, and fronted with panelled pilasters ; it is surmounted by an entablature. In front are the bishop's curious arms, which occur more distinctly in the glass of the north choir aisle—Per fess, in chief a demi-eagle with two heads and sans wings issuing from a demi-rose conjoined to a demi-sun in splendour in base. On the frieze is the inscription—*preache . thov . the . worde . be . fervent . in . season . and . ovt . of . season . reprove . rebvke . exhorte . w^t . all . longe . svfferyng . & . doctryne . 2 . Timō.* A board along the top, covered with red baize, impairs its beauty at present.

The Lectern, which stands near, is composed of a massive
double desk, surmounted by ornamental work, containing the
arms of the see. It rests upon a ball and turned stem and base,
and is entirely of brass. Bishop Creyghton, who had it made
when he was yet dean, inscribed it on both desks with his
arms and this legend :—*Dr. Rob*ᵗ· *Creyghton upon his returne
from fifteen years Exile, w*ᵗʰ *o*ʳ *Soveraigne Lord Kinge Charles*

Dawkes & Partridge, Photo.]
SUGAR'S CHAPEL—THE LECTERN AND PULPIT.

*y*ᵉ *2*ᵈ· *made Deane of wells, in y*ᵉ *yeare 1660, gave this Brazen
Deske, w*ᵗʰ *God's holy worde thereon to the saide Cathedrall
Church.* The Bible referred to still rests upon it, bearing the
same date ; it is bound up with the Prayer Book, and contains initial letters and a frontispiece, but it stops at the
book of Job.

Opposite the lectern are two sixteenth-century panelled
wooden stalls, with round finials, all bearing the same device
on both sides—a Tudor rose with *I.H.S.* in the centre, and the

letters *m.d.l.i.i.* (1552) on the five petals. These *excellent examples of simple and effective woodwork were found amongst some lumber in 1846, and now form part of the temporary choir stalls that are used for the nave services.

On the south side of Bubwith's chapel, and partly covered by it, is a slab, 10 ft. long, covering the grave of Bishop Haselshaw, with the inscription, *Walterus de Haselshaw Ep.* 1308. On the west of Sugar's chapel, another slab bears the inscription, *Radulphus Erghum Ep.* 1401. In a slab near the entrance to the choir there is the matrix for a brass of a lady, with mitred head-dress of the period, *c.* 1460, beneath a canopy. The style suggests that it may belong to Lady Lisle, whose tomb possibly stood here.

The Transepts are both of the same architectural character, and were evidently built before the nave. They have less ornament, the medallions and the carved tympana of the nave being alike absent, although there are the same small heads at the angles of the pier arches. The triforium, too, is different; each bay consists of two large openings, devoid of ornament, instead of three narrower ones, and is separated from the next bay by the vaulting-shaft which reaches down to the string-course of the pier arch (see p. 77). Some of the carved work, however, of the capitals and corbels is of a later date than that of the nave, which may be due to the capitals having been left uncut till after the nave was finished, or to damage done by the fall of the *tholus* in 1248. Apparently the corbels of the vaulting shafts are later than those of the nave, they are certainly more elaborate. Of the capitals those on the west side of both transepts are of one style, and abound in representations of the toothache. The capitals on the east side are different from those on the west of the third pier on this side of the south transept, and that is of a style that suggests the Decorated period. Those on the west are certainly the best, and some of the following are the finest in the church, and perhaps in England :—

North Transept, *first Pier.*—(Inside the Priest Vicars' vestry) A prophet (?) with scroll on which there is no name : Man carrying goose. (Outside) Head with tongue on teeth.

Second Pier.—Aaron, writing his name on a scroll : Moses with the tables of stone.

Third Pier. — Woman with a bandage across her face.

Above this cap the corbel consists of a seated figure, naked, with distorted mouth and an agonised expression.

South Transept, *second Pier* (from the south end).—

SECTION OF N. TRANSEPT AND ELEVATION OF S. TRANSEPT.

Two men are stealing grapes, one holds the basket full, the other plucks grapes, holding a knife in his other hand : The farmers in pursuit, one carries a spade and the other a pitchfork : The man with the fork, a vigorous figure, catches one thief : The man with the spade hits the other (whose face is most woe-begone) on the head (illust. p. 79).

Third Pier.—Woman pulling thorn out of her foot : Man with one eye, finger in his mouth : Baboon head : Cobbler ; this figure shows very plainly the method of shoemaking at this time ; the cobbler, in his apron, sits with the shoe on one knee, his strap passes over the knee and round the other foot, his foot is turned over so as to present the side and not the sole to the strap : Woman's head with long hair.

Fourth Pier. — Head perfectly hairless : " Elias P." (the prophet) with hand on cheek as if he too has the toothache : Head in hood, with tongue on the one remaining tooth.

It may be well here to say a word about the general classification of these earlier capitals, since their date is a matter of great architectural interest. I would venture to divide them into five groups—

1. Those of the three western bays of the choir : simple carved foliage of distinctly Norman character, as in the north porch : these belong to the time of Reginald (1174-1191).

2. The four eastern bays of the nave and its aisles. Some of these may belong to the first period, though later than the choir : they are more advanced in the foliage, and teem with grotesque birds and beasts. Some, however, of the caps in these bays are of quite different character (p. 80) ; they contain *genre* subjects of perfectly naturalistic treatment, very different to the St. Edmund of the north porch capital, but exactly similar to the figure caps of the transepts. They must therefore have been carved later than the death of Saint William Bytton.

3. The western bays of the nave. These, which are of much less interest, belong to the period of Jocelin's reconstruction (1220-1242). They are characteristic examples of rich stiff-leaf foliage, freer than that of the earlier work, but much less varied and without either human figures or grotesques.

4. On the eastern range of transept piers. These would seem also to come within Jocelin's period, with the exception of the third pier of the south transept.

5. On the western range of transept piers (p. 89), with which must be classed those later caps already referred to in the nave under group 2. Their date is settled by the

fact that they abound in unmistakable representations of the toothache. Now Saint William Bytton died in 1274, and his tomb became immediately famous for cures of this malady. In 1286 the chapter decided to repair the old work, no doubt because the offerings at his tomb had brought money to the church; this part of the church had been damaged ever since the fall of the *tholus* in 1248.

T. W. Phillips, Photo.]

CAPITALS IN TRANSEPT.

The caps must therefore have been carved during the episcopate of Burnell (1275-1292). Mr Irvine, indeed, suggests that the figure of the woman taking a thorn ("bur") from her foot may contain a reference to Bishop Burnell. The undercroft passage, with its curious corbels and bosses, was probably also a part of the old work then completed, as it contains one "toothache" head. Although the introduction of such finished figure-subjects into the capitals suggests this lateness of date, they are still completely Early

THE SOUTH TRANSEPT FROM NORTH SIDE OF NAVE.

English in style, and a great gulf is fixed between them
and the Decorated caps of the chapter-house begun by
Burnell's successor, William de Marchia (1293-1302).

The Font is of peculiar interest as the one surviving
relic of Bishop Robert's Norman church. Whether it also
stood in the still earlier Saxon church is still an open
question : it is as likely
to be of pre-Norman as
of Norman date, and
the fact that whatever
ornament there may have
been in the spandrels of
its shallow arcades has
been hacked off, makes
conjecture unsafe. Its
unusual position in the
south transept may be
due to the Bishop Giso's
quasi-conventual build-
ings on the south of the
church, which would
have made this transept
the most common en-
trance to the cathedral
at the time of the Con-
quest. A Jacobean
cover rests upon the
font, and with it forms
a charming combination
of pre-Gothic and post-
Gothic Romanesque
design.

THE FONT.
(Drawn by W. Heywood.)

At the south end of
the south transept is
the tomb of Bishop *de
Marchia* (*ob.* 1302). The effigy lies in a recess, and is
covered with a canopy of three bays, the ogival arches,
finished in sumptuous crockets and finials, painted red
and gold, the spandrels being alternately green and red,
powdered with a little pattern, the cusps and mouldings
scarlet and crimson and green and gold, with a dark colour

in the shadows. The effigy of the bishop is one of the best in the cathedral, but even more lovely are the three little figures so charmingly supported on foliage at the back of the tomb—two angels and a bishop between them. The heads of these three figures have been wickedly destroyed, but parts of the chains of the angels' censers remain. Of the two beautiful angels which hold the cushion the heads fortunately remain. Along the plinth of the tomb are six heads which are quite unique in their treatment; three are bearded (one of these is bald); one is shaven, tonsured, and turned half round in a strangely naturalistic manner; another is also shaven, and the remaining head is that of a woman in a veil. Two large faces are carved on the east and west ends of the tomb, both with long wavy hair—one of a woman, the other with a wavy beard. The central boss of the vaulting is carved with five roses, which are coloured green, their foliage, like all the foliage in this tomb, being gilt on a red ground with the red edges showing. The little angels at the back had gilded robes with red lining, and blue wings; the little bishop wore a red chasuble with green (or blue) dalmatic, and red tunicle over his white alb; the lappets of his mitre, which have survived, were red, and traces of dark blue are on his shoes: there seem to have been patterns on the various vestments, and the colours can still be seen where their sleeves overlapped. Modern lettering has been cut across the back of the tomb and coloured, by way of contrast to the ancient work.

Under the battlemented cornice of the curtain-wall to the west a row of heads is painted in fresco on a red ground, which seems to be part of the same scheme with the curious heads on the plinth of de Marchia's tomb: one of these, a woman in a dark-coloured hood, is especially distinct. No doubt the whole wall was originally painted. The sill of the window over the tomb seems to have been used for some special purpose: there is a passage cut through the splay of the window, through which the sill may be reached, which is not the case with the corresponding window of the north transept. The passage is reached from a staircase concealed behind the curtain-wall, which is reached by an ogee-headed doorway (with cusps in the head, finial, and two small heads to its very beautiful mouldings). This staircase also leads to a chamber on the level of the passage, but on the west side: the interior of the chamber can be seen from the ground, as its old wooden door is kept open. It is supposed by some to have been a watching chamber in connection with the tomb. There can, indeed, be little doubt that these arrangements had something to do with de Marchia's tomb, or that the ornamented doorway in the curtain wall of the same date as the tomb, together with the frescoes on the wall, were connected with the strong efforts that were made at this time for his canonisation. Perhaps the sill was used for the display of his relics, and the chamber was the ordinary resting-place of the reliquary, for which purpose the door and the absence of windows would have fitted it.

Next to de Marchia's tomb on the other side, the monument of Joan Viscountess *Lisle* (*ob.* 1463) gives a good illustration of the change of architecture in a hundred and fifty years. The crockets are less free, and straight lines and square members abound; the fine ogee curve of its single arch is weakened by the rather weedy cusps, its shafts have become tiny mouldings, and their capitals mere knops. It is coloured, too, all over, in green and red and yellow, but heavily in comparison with its neighbour. The colour has been unusually well preserved, owing to the fact that the tomb was plastered over, and not discovered till 1809. There is no effigy, but a brass of apparently recent date bears this inscription:— *Hic jacet Joanna Vicecomitilla de Lisle una filiarum et haeredum Thomae Chedder, armiger quae fuit uxor Joannis Vicecomitis de Lisle, filii et haeredis Joannis Comitis Salopiæ et Margaretæ ux ejus unius filiarum et haeredum Ricardi comitis Warwici et Elizabethae uxoris ejus filiæ et haeredis Thomæ de Berkley militis, domini de Berkeley, quæ obiit xvᵐᵒ die mensis Julii Ann Dⁱ MCCCCLXIII.* Lady Lisle's husband was killed at the battle of Chastillon (1453), when he was serving under his father, the famous Earl of Shrewsbury. The painted designs above the three niches should be noticed, and also those of the moulding and fleurs-de-lys at the side. The monument was evidently used as a chantry chapel; but it did not originally stand here. The brass by the north side of the screen (p. 89) may mark the site.

The eastern aisles of the transepts are divided off into chapels by two Perpendicular stone screens, that of the south transept having a doorway in it for each chapel. These chapels are thus dedicated, beginning from the south—St. Martin, St. Calixtus, St. David, Holy Cross. From the last-named chapel the chapter-house is reached through an Early English doorway, and a similar doorway (now partly blocked by Biconyll's tomb) led from St. Martin's to a small building, supposed to have been a vestry, which once stood outside. In the south transept there are also—a small door to the tower, a small door with ogee head (p. 96), a rather larger doorway with modern lintel leading to the library (two shafts just above this door have been cut off, and faces very roughly cut on their extremities by way of corbel), and the large doorway leading to the cloister. The principal windows belong to the original work, having been merely filled with Perpendicular tracery. The windows of the south-east aisle contain Decorated tracery, but the tracery of the north-east aisle is not good.

The western aisle of the south transept is open ; that of the north transept is cut off by a Perpendicular stone screen, which is solid in the southern bay, and through carved in the northern. The latter is, however, boarded up, and used as the vestry of the priest-vicars, the other being the vestry of the vicars-choral. From the priest-vicars' vestry a door leads into a small chamber now used for the water supply, and over the doorway there is a small and pretty figure of a woman under a little niche.

There are a very few fragments of Early Perpendicular glass in some of the upper lights of the nave and transept windows. There are also two modern windows at the west end of the nave, and one in the south transept, of which I have been unable to discover the actual designers' names.

Transept Chapels.—**St. Martin's**, where the obits of Savaric and Jocelin were celebrated, is separated by a solid Perpendicular screen from the adjoining chapel of St. Calixtus. It is now used as the canons' vestry. Partly blocking the old Early English doorway is the tomb of *Biconyll*, who was chancellor in 1454. His will, with a good deal of information about him, is given in the *Somerset Proceedings* for 1894, by Mr A. S. Bicknell, a descendant. The name was originally Byken-hulle (A.S. for Beacon Hill), and has been spelt in forty-seven different ways. His effigy lies on the tomb, dressed in cassock, long surplice, and *cappa nigra* or choral cope. The ends of the almuce can be seen in the opening of the cope, and its hood hangs over the shoulders.

St. Calixtus' chapel is enclosed on the side of the choir aisle by part of the beautiful ironwork from Beckington's tomb. The doors of this and St. Martin's chapel are also made from the same iron screen. Within the chapel, and near the screen, in strange contrast to it, stands one of those indescribable stoves which disfigure the church, its chimney, as usual, driven through the vault. The east end of the chapel is occupied by the canopy which formed part of Bishop *Beckington's* tomb till the restoration of 1850, when it was, by an inexcusable act of vandalism, taken down and fixed up in this place (p. 125). This canopy did not cover the tomb, but stood at its foot so as to form the eastern part of a chantry chapel, the tomb being on its south side and the iron screen enclosing it where it jutted into the choir on the north side. It will be noticed that its northern angle was sloped off so as not to present an awkward corner on the side of the choir. The reredos, for such it really is, is a most elaborate and charming piece of work; "pretty" is perhaps the word that describes it best, if "pretty" be taken in its very best sense. Here there is nothing of the suave grace of de Marchia's tomb, nothing of the vigour and truth of the transept capitals, nothing of the noble delicacy of the north porch, which was a delicacy of intellect, while this is a delicacy of execution. It is certainly decadent; even by the side of Sugar's chapel it is over-refined and a thought effeminate, but, with the colour that still covers it fresh and bright, it must have had all the fascination of a splendid piece of jewellery, where profusion of ornament is more desired than structural grace. The cornice is particularly rich with a finely-carved vine ornament, and with two angels, their long outstretched wings minutely feathered, who bear shields having representations of the sacred wounds. The tabernacle work behind the altar is gone, like the altar itself, with the exception of the small niches which formed the sides of the central composition, but the little canopy of the central niche remains to give us a slight idea of its workmanship. The short wings of the reredos have panels and traceried openings, and, on the south, a piscina

which looks almost too tiny to be real. The top has a toy
like vault of fan-tracery with little pendants.

On the south side of St. Calixtus' chapel is *Dean Husse's*
alabaster tomb (*ob.* 1305), which bears some of the best
carved work in the cathedral. The effigy itself is good: it
represents the Dean clad in the same choir vestments as the
figures on the panels below. These panels should on no
account be missed. The first on the left represents the
Annunciation with a grace that is not less delightful for the
strain of exaggeration which pervades it. The Blessed Virgin
(see illustration on p. 101), a lovely figure in long, close-fitting
kirtle and mantle thrown gracefully over her shoulders, turns
round from the desk at which she is kneeling, and throws out
her arms with a quaint gesture of surprise; her crown and
nimbus are both of enormous size. A very small Gabriel
dashes down from the top corner, bearing a scroll which takes
up the whole of the panel; he is preceded by a Dove with
very long rays. The next three panels (passing over these
with shields) contain three figures of clergy, two of which hold
books, and all their short staves. They wear the cassock, long
surplice, and a long, graceful choral cope, somewhat like the
modern academic gown in shape, the rounded ends of the
hooded almuce reach to the knee and are held at the chest
by a cord with tassels. There is no better representation of
medieval choir vestments in existence than these three figures.
The last panel is a curious representation of the Eternal
Father holding the crucifix; this remarkable figure has a *very*
long face, great masses of curly hair, a huge crown, and
very long hands.

The two chapels of the north transept can only be reached
through the choir aisle, no doubt because the way to the
chapter-house was through them. The first was probably
St David's chapel. Here should be noticed the capital of
the easternmost shaft of the second transept pier—a head
with curly hair and handsome smiling face. This shaft is
corbelled off, and the corbel through carved in the shape of
a lizard eating the leaves of a plant with berries thereon; it
is a charming study. The tomb of Bishop *Still* (1543-1607)
in this chapel is under a handsome canopy of warm-coloured
marbles, with black columns and red, blue, and gold decoration.
The effigy is dressed in rochet and chimere, over which is a red

robe lined with white fur; a ruff is round the neck, a close-fitting black cap covers the head and part of the ears, and the rochet is finished at the wrists with a plain black band.

In the chapel of the **Holy Cross** the monument of the intruding Bishop *Kidder*, Ken's successor (p. 158, *ob.* 1703), stands on the site of the altar, whither it has been removed from its original position on the south side of the choir. Standing in all its chilly pretentiousness so near to Still's tomb, it well illustrates the immense decline in monumental art which took place during the seventeenth century. The bishop's daughter, who erected the monument, is represented reclining, as, with one arm outstretched, she looks at two urns which are supposed to contain the ashes of her father and mother; underneath is a very long Latin inscription.

Against the north wall and close to the entrance to the chapter-house stands the tomb of Bishop *Cornish* (*ob.* 1513). He was chancellor and precentor of Wells, and suffragan bishop under Bishop Fox of Bath and Wells and Bishop Oldham

T. W. Phillips, Photo.]
THE ANNUNCIATION.
(Husse's Tomb.)

of Exeter, his title being Bishop of Tenos. Part of the inscription remains :—*Obiit supradictus dũs Thomas Tinensis Epũs tercio die mensis Julii anno. . . . MCCCCCXIII Cujus Anime p [ropitietur Deus A] m e n.* The three panels on the front bear shields—**T** with a sheaf of corn, Cornish's arms (on a chevron between three birds' heads erased a mitre) and **C** with a sheaf of corn ; on the side panel are the arms of the chapter, the arms, that is, of the see without the pastoral staff.   Against the wall within the canopy are some matrices of small brasses, in which the kneeling figure of a bishop, a scroll, and two plates for inscriptions can be traced.

T. W. Phillips, Photo.]

PRIEST IN SURPLICE.
(Husse's Tomb.)

From several peculiarities in Cornish's tomb, I am convinced that it was also used as the *Easter Sepulchre*, where the Host was laid during the concluding days of Holy Week.   These sepulchres were often made in connection with a tomb, and the usual place for them was somewhere on the north side of the choir.   The position here in the chapel of the Holy Cross (which is an appropriate dedication) would be particularly convenient for the purpose.   The chapel was easily reached by the clergy without their having to go into the public part of the church ; it was thus as safe a place as the choir itself, and at the same time was much more open to the people, who could pay their devotions from the transept, and through the open stone screen could see the candles burning round the sepulchre.

Just where it could be best seen from the transept, on the
eastern end of the upper storey of the tomb under the canopy,

THE EAST END IN 1823.

is a carving of the Resurrection. A wide arch is cut in the
stone; within this is carved a square opening, not through-cut,

but farther recessed, to represent the mouth of the sepulchre; in front of the square recess is the figure of Christ, issuing from the tomb, clad only in a long mantle, which He holds across His body; the hair is long, the face mutilated, and the hands gone. At the left is the kneeling figure of a bishop, the head gone, but part of the staff remaining in the hands. There is a great crack (now filled with mortar) round these two figures, as if the attack of the iconoclasts had been made with heavy tools. A pedestal at the right-hand corner of the square recess seems a later insertion, as it is loose and does not exactly fit; probably it was added soon after the tomb was made, to hold a small silver figure of an angel, or of a soldier, as there is a little hole (now filled with mortar) at a height above it convenient for rivetting a metal figure.

The Sepulchre proper would have consisted of a small coped chest, in shape like a reliquary, round which would be painted the incidents of the Passion. The slab of the tomb, being without the usual recumbent effigy, would have formed the place on which this "coffer" rested, this being the usual method when a tomb was used for the purpose. On Good Friday, the Host, often in a specially-made pyx, was with much ceremony laid in the coffer, together with the altar-cross, and there was kept, surrounded by candles and guarded by watchers, till Easter Day. We know that there was a special provision at Wells for one candle to burn continuously within the Sepulchre "*I cereus in sepulchro cum corpori Dominico qui continue ardebit donec Matutinae cantentur in die Paschae*" *MS. Harl.* 1682, *fo.* 5). There is a small hole in the east wall of this chapel, close to the tomb and a little below the level of of the slab whereon the coffer would have rested; this may have held a sconce or some ornament. But the *cereus in sepulchro* was probably a large candle within the chapel, and in accordance with general usage, there would have been other candles burning upon cressets. There are two other holes in the north wall, a few inches to the east of the top of the tomb, which may have held rods for the curtains that were used in much profusion for the adornment of Easter sepulchres. While the coffer stood on the slab it would have hidden the carving of the Resurrection; but on its removal on Easter Day, the carving would have stood in full view of the people, bright, no doubt, with colour and surrounded by lights. It will further be noticed that the tomb stands eighteen inches away from the east wall, the space being now filled with modern masonry; this was probably in order to leave ample room for the sacred ministers in their vestments; had it stood close against the wall the ceremonial could not have been conveniently carried out.

Near the tomb is the doorway, with a fine old oak door, which leads into the chapter-house; and above the tomb is a window which was blocked up when the vestibule was built, and a bracket set in the masonry.

The Clock is a great favourite with visitors, who generally congregate in the north transept at the striking of the hour and laugh gently to one another when the quaint performance is over. "Jack Blandiver" (this is the name given him by the country people for some undiscovered reason) kicks his bell at each quarter in the most life-like manner, his feet trembling afterwards with the exertion; but at the hour, after Jack has sounded his four quarters, as the big bell begins to toll, the four "knights" above the clock rush round in contrary directions, and charge each other with so much ferocity that one unfortunate is felled at each encounter, and has barely time to recover his upright position before he is again and again knocked down with resounding clatter upon his horse's back. The other three fight twenty-four times a day unscathed.

The clock was thus described by Mr Octavius Morgan, F.R.S., in the *Archæological Journal* for 1883:

"In the Cathedral of Wells is what remains of the ancient clock which once belonged to Glastonbury Abbey. This very curious timepiece is said to have been originally executed by Peter Lightfoot, a monk of the abbey, but at the cost of Adam de Sodbury, who was promoted to the abbacy in 1322. It appears to have been originally placed in the south transept of Glastonbury Abbey Church, where it continued till the Dissolution, when, tradition says, it was carried to Wells and placed in the north transept of the cathedral with all its belongings—viz. the figure which strikes the quarters with his heels on two little bells within the church, and the two "knights" which perform the same service with their battle axes on the outside. The inside figure strikes the hour on a bell before him with a battle-axe in his hands. The face of the dial is 6 feet in diameter, contained in a square frame, the spandrels of which are filled with angels holding in their hands the head of a man ; the outer circle is painted blue, with gilt stars scattered over it, and is divided into twenty-four parts, corresponding with the twenty-four hours ; the horary numbers are in black-letter characters on circular tablets, and mark the hours from twelve at noon to midnight, and from thence to midnight again (noon and midnight being marked by a cross instead of a numeral). The hour index, a large gilt star or sun, is attached to the machinery behind a second circle which conceals all except the index. On the second circle are marked the minutes, indicated by a smaller star ; a third and lesser circle contains the numbers of the days of the month, which is marked by a point attached to a small circular opening in the plate, through which the phases of the moon are shown. On the opposite side is a female figure, with the motto *Semper peragrat Phœbe*.

"An arched pediment surmounts the whole, with an octagonal projection from its base like a gallery, capped with a row of battlements, forming a cornice to the face of the clock. A panelled and battlemented turret is fixed in the centre, round which four figures mounted on horses revolve in opposite directions, as if charging at a tournament, when set in motion by a communication with the clockwork, to be made at pleasure ; these are commonly called *knights*, but their costume is only that of ordinary persons. The movement is at a distance from the dial, and connected with it by a long horizontal rod ; the dial work was close at the back of the dial. The revolving figures on horseback are moved by a separate weight, and are set in motion by the freeing of a detent. The old boarding at the back [in the vestry of the vicars-choral] is painted black, with a diaper scroll of foliage with red and white roses. The female figure on the dial, representing the moon, is always kept upright by a balance weight ; the quarter-boys inside, who strike the quarters, are much later, having *knee-breeches*.

"The outside dial has now two hands ; it was once like a star with only one hand. The bells outside are struck by two figures in armour, *temp*. Henry VIII., probably put up when it was removed from Glastonbury.

"The clock seems to have remained without alteration

after it was then put up, till the present modern movement, made by Thwaites & Reed of Clerkenwell, was, in the time of Dean Goodenough, substituted for it, and the old original movement was taken and deposited in the crypt under the chapter-house, where it remained uncared for, for many years, during which time, 1853, I visited and examined it, made notes of it, and took drawings of it. The great wheel has ninety teeth, and the pinion, a lantern-pinion, had nine leaves, or rather bars; the second wheel had sixty teeth; the remainder of the works were all disjointed and bent, and remained unheeded." The whole is now fitted together, and in a going condition, in the mechanical museum at South Kensington.

The *Antiquary* for August 1897 ("Some Mediaeval Mechanicians") reminds us that, as the clock was in constant use at Glastonbury for about 250 years, and then at Wells for another 250 years, and as the old movement is now still working at the South Kensington, "as though its life were interminable"—it is probably the oldest piece of working mechanism extant.

The same article says of these old works: "It will give an idea of the labour involved, when it is stated the mechanism of the clock occupies a space of about 5 feet cube (125 cubic feet), that the structure is wholly of forged iron; that the numerous wrought-iron wheels, some of which are nearly 2 feet in diameter and about $\frac{1}{2}$ inch thick, besides having to be made truly circular and concentric, had all their teeth cut out and trimmed to workable shape by hand; and that the heavy wrought-iron frames, etc., are fastened entirely by means of mortise, tenon, and colter, no screws being used in the whole structure. The pinions are of the lantern form, with octagonal cheek-plates on square spindles, and the pendulum of modern form beats seconds."

The Inverted Arches.—Undoubtedly the first thing that the stranger notices in Wells Cathedral, and the last that he is likely to forget, is the curious contrivance by which the central tower is supported. Of the three pairs of arches (the upper arch resting inverted upon the lower) which stretch across the nave and each of the transepts, that in the nave is seen at once, and lends a unique character to the whole church. At first these arches give one something of a shock, so unnecessarily frank are they, so excessively sturdy, so very English, we may think. They carry their burden as a great-limbed labourer will carry a child in a crowd, to the great advantage of the burden, and the natural dissatisfaction of the crowd. In fact, they seem to block up the view, and to deform what they do not hide.

That is the first impression, but it does not last for long. Familiarity breeds respect for this simple, strong device, which arrested the fall of the tower in the fourteenth century, and has kept its walls ever since in perfect security, so that the great structure has stood like a rock upon the watery soil of Wells for nearly seven centuries, with its rents and breaks just as they were when the damage was first repaired. The ingenuity, too, of these strange flying buttresses becomes more and more evident; the "ungainly props" are seen to be so worked into the tower they support, that they almost seem like part of the original design of the first builders. One discovers that it is the organ, and not the arches, that really blocks the view, and one marvels that so huge a mass of masonry can look so light as to present, with the great circles in the spandrels where the arches meet, "a kind of pattern of gigantic geometrical tracery." Indeed, I think no one who has been in Wells a week could wish to see the inverted arches removed.

Professor Willis, who had made a most careful investigation of the masonry, thus describes the cause and the construction of the inverted arches (*Somerset Proceedings*, 1863, i. 21) : "It is evident that the weight of the upper storey of the tower completed in 1321 had produced fearful settlements, the effects of which may still be seen in the triforium arches of the nave, and transepts next to the tower, which are dragged downwards and deformed, partly rebuilt, filled up, and otherwise exhibiting the signs so often seen under central towers, of a thorough repair. The great piers of the tower are cased and connected by a stone framework, which is placed under the north, south, and west tower-arches, but not under the east. This framework consists of a low pointed arch, upon which rests an inverted arch of the same form, so as to produce a figure somewhat resembling a St. Andrew's cross, to use the happy phrase applied by Leland to a similar contrivance introduced for a similar reason [but at a later date] into the central tower arches of Glastonbury." To this description there only needs to be added a mention of the circles which occupy the spandrels, and help to prevent the whole structure from seeming a mere inert mass of masonry. To appreciate the work fully, it should be looked at from some spot, such as the north-east corner of the north transept, whence the three great pairs of arches can be seen together. The effect from here is very fine, especially when the nave is lighted up, and strong shadows are cast. The extreme boldness of the mouldings, the absence of shafts and capitals and of all ornament, give them a primitive vigour, and their great intermingling curves, which contrast so magnificently with the little shafts of the piers beyond, seem more like a part of some great mountain cavern than a mere device of architectural utility.

Dawkes & Partridge, Photo.]

THE INVERTED ARCHES, FROM THE
NORTH TRANSEPT.

At the same time as the arches were built, flying buttresses were inserted further to secure the tower, and they can be seen blocking up the triforium and clerestory of those bays, in nave, choir, and transepts, which adjoin it. Other repairs were necessary, for the pier-arches of the same bays in nave and transepts were completely shattered, and had to be replaced by the present ones, the queer-looking capitals of which contrast so oddly with the earlier work. It is instructive, also, to compare the lightness of these fourteenth-century mouldings with the boldness of those, wrought at exactly the same time, of the great inverted arches.

The Tower.—Besides its inverted arches and other signs of repair, the tower is mainly noticeable for its Perpendicular fan-tracery vault of fifteenth-century date. This vault hides the lantern with its arcades, and thus destroys one of the elements of distance and mystery which, before the advent of the more prosaic Perpendicular period, had been a characteristic of Gothic architecture. Nothing else but the desire for uniformity can account for this unjustifiable addition ; for there can have been no intention of hanging bells in the lantern when there were already two western bell-towers. The lantern, with its cracked masonry, can be seen during the ascent of the tower (p. 47).

The shafts of the eastern tower arches were corbelled off at some height from the ground, in order to allow the stalls of the first ritual choir to be set flat against the wall. This shows that Bishop Reginald, when he rebuilt the church, kept to the old Romanesque arrangement and made his choir under the tower, reserving his three bays of what is now the choir for the presbytery—a very dignified arrangement. The square holes for fixing the wooden screen of this earlier choir can still be traced on the aisle walls in a line with the ninth piers of the nave.

The Screen was built in the fourteenth century ; but Salvin altered and spoilt it by bringing forward the middle portion to carry the unsightly organ. Mr Freeman objected very strongly to the choir being shut off from the nave by this screen, and urged the authorities to pull it down and throw the whole church open from end to end. The remedy suggested by Mr St. John Hope, on the other hand, is that a second screen should be erected under the western arch of the tower, against which the nave or rood altar should stand, with seats for the choir on either side. Such a screen as this was certainly used in conventual churches, and would be more in accord with the spirit of medieval architecture, which was content to sacrifice the grandeur of great space in order to gain the qualities of seclusion and mystery, and inexhaustible variety.

Two things, at least, are certain. The long-established custom of crowding the Sunday congregation into the choir should be abolished, and the organ should be modified or removed. Magnificent Sunday services could be held in the

CHOIR, LOOKING WEST.

nave, either with a second screen and altar or without a screen
at all ; but, as the former plan could be tried without any
destruction of old work, it should be tried first.

As for the organ, the cathedral will always be defaced while
it remains as a whole in the midst of the screen. Musical
experts could no doubt distribute it so that it would no longer
be an offence to the eye, and yet would sound more effectively
than at present. Perhaps galleries for the swell, pedal, and
great organs might be built above the pier-arches in the western
bay of the choir on either side, and the consol, with the choir
organ, might remain on the screen. Some fragments of tabernacle work on the triforium level would thus be hidden, but it is
unremarkable work, exactly similar to that of the adjoining bays,
and, moreover, it was so blocked and patched when the tower
was strengthened that it would not be a disadvantage to hide it.
As it is, the organ, unsightly in shape, and garishly painted,
blocks up the view of the splendid east window, and makes
the nave a mere vestibule to the choir. The inverted arches
are generally thought to block up the church, but were the
organ removed it would be found that they do not.

The Organ is a modern instrument by Willis. Dean
Creyghton, a musician whose services are still sung in the
cathedral, built the old organ in 1664, and S. Green of London
repaired it in 1786, but only one diapason remains of the old
stops. The case also disappeared, the present one being
among the ugliest in England. There are three manuals ;
thirteen speaking stops on the great organ, ten on the swell,
nine on the choir, and eight on the pedal organ. The swell
organ is rather small, but has been recently improved ; the
pedal organ is the best feature of the instrument. The wind
is supplied by hydraulic machinery. There are four pneumatic
pistons, six couplers, and seven composition pedals. The
organist now sits on the south side, so that he can see his
choristers, whether they sing in the choir or the nave.

The Choir.—The western part of the choir should be
particularly noticed. For, while the three eastern bays which
form the presbytery are Late Decorated, the three western bays
of the choir are twelfth-century work of Bishop Reginald's
time, being, in fact, the oldest part of the interior. That they
were finished before Reginald's other work in the transepts and
nave is not only likely from the general custom of medieval

architects, but is made probable by the carving of the capitals, which is less advanced than that in any other part of the church.

It will be noticed, however, that, though the three arches remain of the earlier bays, the two easternmost *piers* of the old part are Decorated, like those in the three later bays ; and some of their arch mouldings have been cut away in order to fit the new capitals. The reason for this peculiar combination of a new pier with an old arch is an interesting one. The original pier marked the east end of Reginald's church, and it was taken from under its arch because, being at the junction of the east wall with the side walls, it was a large compound pier quite unfitted to stand as one of an arcade. The three bays then formed the presbytery of the church, and the choir was placed, Norman fashion, under the tower. A further evidence of this being the original east end of the church is presented by the two early buttresses outside at this point, which are much wider than any of the others. But there must have been an ambulatory beyond the east end of the old church, since Reginald's work is carried a bay farther east in the choir aisles. There may, too, have been a small chapel beyond.

Speaking of the contrast between the three early bays and the later work, Freeman says : "The new work, though exceedingly graceful, is perhaps too graceful ; it has a refinement and minuteness of detail which is thoroughly in place in a small building like the Lady Chapel, but which gives a sort of feeling of weakness when it is transferred to a principal part of the church of the full height of the building. The three elder arches are all masculine vigour ; the three newer arches are all feminine elegance ; but it strikes me that feminine elegance, thoroughly in its place in the small chapels, is hardly in its place in the presbytery."

Certainly, the mouldings of the later arches will not bear comparison with those of the earlier. The suave strength of the transitional mouldings forms a most instructive contrast to the less effective minuteness of the decadent work. The same is true of the capitals : those of the later period have little architectural significance, and many of them are further weakened by the fact that not the capital only, but the adjoining part of the shaft as well, is cut out of white stone.

With the exception, however, of the three pier-arches them-

CHOIR, LOOKING EAST.
PROCESSION PATH AND LADY PATH BEYOND.

selves, there are few signs of the twelfth-century work. For, when the new presbytery was finished, the clerestory over the old arches was altered, and the triforium cased with tabernacle work (though not in quite so rich a style), so as to bring them into harmony with the fourteenth-century work, and to fit them to carry the new vault. The tabernacle work of the presbytery must have been completed first ; for no attempt was made to keep it at the same level with the old part, which, when the builders determined to adapt it to the new, caused a very marked break at the juncture.

There is, strictly speaking, no triforium, the space being occupied by the rather florid tabernacle work, the effect of which is, of course, considerably impaired by the absence of statuary. The niches in the presbytery are deeper than those in the choir ; they spring direct from the pier-arches, having no spandrel, and they contain richly-foliated brackets, which rest on triple shafts. This part is also marked by triple vaulting shafts of Purbeck, which are carried down to the floor.

The clerestory windows contain flowing tracery of an advanced and not very good type. In some the plain mullions are carried on through the head of the window and intersect each other.

Above the tabernacle work of the east end is the east window of seven lights, the last bit of the fourteenth-century reconstruction, the last flicker of Decorated freedom. Its curious tracery is still beautiful, doubly so for the glass it enshrines, but the rule and square of Perpendicular domination have already set their mark upon it ; the two principal mullions run straight up to the window-head, and part of the tracery between them is rectangular.

The inhabitants of Wells are, or were, exceedingly proud of the " vista " into the procession-path and Lady Chapel, which is afforded by the three dainty pointed arches of the east end. So proud were they that they would suffer nothing to stand behind the high altar but a low stone wall, barely higher than the altar itself, an arrangement which, it is hardly necessary to point out, defeated its own end by reducing the whole effect to absolute baldness. Mr Freeman wisely pointed out the need of a respectable reredos, remarking that the original founders never dreamed of the Lady Chapel acting as a " peep-show to the choir." A Lady Chapel, he added, was built specially not to be peeped into, but to be a thing apart from the great whole of the church, from the high altar westward. After a while, a reredos was offered to the church, and approved by Mr J. D. Sedding, who was then the cathedral architect; but there was much opposition, and the scheme was dropped. Dean Plumptre, with characteristic temerity, went so far as to appeal to the witness of the *vox populi* that the open view was the best. Since then, wiser counsels have prevailed, and a curtain (small and dingy, it is true, but still a curtain) now hangs behind the altar. While giving a measure of dignity to the east end, it, of course, emphasises, as every architect must have known that it would, the charm of the "peep" into the chapels beyond.

A larger reredos would further enhance the peculiar charm of the east end. There can, indeed, be little doubt that the ancient reredos was of tabernacle work, so as to carry on the effect of niches of the triforium storey. Their present disconnectedness can be no part of the original plan, and a reredos full of statues, which was high enough to group adequately with the rich canopies above could have been the only way to secure dignity and unity of effect. Till an architect is found capable of mastering so delicate a problem of proportion as such a reredos must present, we may well be content with a larger and brighter curtain. The low east wall, with its ugly cresting, warns us not to embark too rashly upon modern stonework.

The lierned stone vault, with its heavy, angular ribs, is of a very unusual kind. Mr Freeman described it as "a coved roof, such as we are used to in woodwork in this part of England, only with cells cut in it for the clerestory windows." The restorers have gilded the bosses, but the space between the ribs is smoothed in a way that gives the appearance of there being no masonry in the construction. One can hardly judge the ceiling, therefore, by its present appearance, which is not further improved by the green wash with which some of the clerestory windows are covered.

The general appearance of the choir suffers pitiably from the ill-advised restoration of 1848 and the following years. Before that time its aspect must have been curious and encumbered; but the judicious removal of the pews and galleries, and the restoration of the truncated oak canopies of the stalls, would have made matters right at a small cost, and without the destruction of any old woodwork. As it was, everything was ruthlessly swept away. The tabernacled stalls, which eighteenth-century vandalism had respected, vanished utterly before the restoring mania of the Gothic revivalist, even their traditional position and order being changed.

The result is just what might have been expected. The place has been completely modernised. Chilly stone canopies cover the stalls; they are of the kind of workmanship which forty years ago was considered excellent. That is to say, they are covered with frigid, ungainly, and pompous ornament, cut with mechanical regularity, and without one trace of feeling or one line of beauty from beginning to end. Below, and between them, the choir is encumbered, much as it was before 1848, with rows of stalls, which are continued in the presbytery almost up to the tawdry brass altar-rails. Two more pale ghosts of medieval art front each other in complacent parody of the work their makers could not even copy—the pulpit and the bishop's throne. The former is Early Victorian; the latter is worse, it is a restoration of Perpendicular work so relentless that not a sign of the original conception remains. Plate-glass fills the tracery at the sides, and the door is a piece of solid swinging stone. On the completion of this terrible work, the restorers seem to have felt dimly the want of colour, which previously had been so abundant. They therefore proceeded to furnish with that peculiar musty red which used to cast a gloom over our childhood—red cushions on the seats, red cushions on the desks, red hassocks on the floor, red edges to the books, hot red in the bishop's throne, dull red on the altar, before the altar, and behind the altar, it is all red but the chilly white stone, and the all-pervading wood-work of the seats, which adds the muddy gloom of oak that has been stained and varnished to the miserable poverty of the whole.

The cause of all this desolation was just the ignorance of its promoters as to the functions of a cathedral. The choir was looked upon as a select church for the leading families of the town, and the seats in it were appropriated; the nave was a vast empty space that was never used for worship at all. Hence the organ on the screen, hence the setting back of the stalls, so that the choir might be widened, and more seats "rammed, jammed, crammed," to use Freeman's indignant words, into the space. Instead of the long continuous range of stalls which formerly existed, there are now groups of five under each arch, with the result that ten of the prebendaries are without accommodation. Such is the heavy legacy of blunders with which the dean and chapter are burdened. It will take many a year before the choir can be redeemed from its unfortunate state; but the present arrangement of the altar is a great improvement on its position only a few years ago, and no doubt similar measures will in time completely efface the traces of 1850.

Of the old woodwork the **Misericords** have alone escaped destruction. Sixty-four of these remain, fifty of which belonged to the prebendal stalls of the upper row, though they were removed from their proper position at the restoration. Sixty of the seats are now in the lower rows of the stalls, the other four are preserved in the library. It is enough to say of them that no finer examples of wood-carving can be seen in England. The following description of the wonderfully fresh and varied subjects was supplied by Mr St. John Hope for a paper read by Canon Church before the *Society of Antiquaries* in March 1896 :—

South side, first row.—1, a goat (broken); 2, a griffin fighting with a lion (?); 3, a man in hood and drawers riding with his face to the tail of a barebacked horse; 4, a hawk preying on a rabbit; 5, a mermaid (unfinished); 6, two popinjays in a fruit tree; 7, an ape carrying a basket of fruit on his back (broken); 8, a double-bodied monster; 9, a dog-headed griffin; 10, two goats butting (unfinished); 11, a monkey holding an owl (unfinished); 12, two dragons interlocked and biting each other's tails; 13, an ewe suckling a lamb (unfinished); 14, a wyvern and a horse fighting. *South side, second row.*—15, a mermaid suckling a lion; 16, a man holding a cup? (broken), sitting on the ground, and disputing with another man holding a pouch; 17, a cat preying on a mouse (unfinished); 18, a monster with bat's wings; 19, a griffin devouring a lamb; 20, a puppy biting a cat; 21, a man in a contorted position upholding the seat; 22, a serious-looking dog; 23, a cat playing a fiddle; 24, a man seated on the ground and thrusting a dagger through the head of a dragon with feathered wings; 25, bust of a bishop, in amice, chasuble, and mitre (unfinished); 26, a peacock in his pride; 27, a fox preaching to four geese, one of which has fallen asleep (broken); 28, a cock crowing. *North side, first row.*—29, a lion dormant; 30, a dragon with expanded wings, asleep; 31, a man with his left eye closed, wearing a cloak and squatting on the ground with his hands on his knees; 32, a fox running off with a goose in his mouth; 33, head of a man with donkey's ears; 34, two monsters with male and female human heads, caressing (unfinished); 35, a man on his back upholding the seat with his right hand and right foot ; 36, a lion with the ears of an ass ; 37, a hawk scratching its head ; 38, a sleeping cat (unfinished) ; 39, a woman with dishevelled hair and agonised expression, crouching on the ground with the right hand on her shoulder, the other extended ; 40, a dragon with hairy belly biting his back ; 41, two ducks addorsed, one with his beak open ; 42, two dragons fighting (unfinished) ; 43, a bat's head (unfinished). *North side, second row.*—44, head of a man with bushy hair and beard, with a lion's leg growing out of each side ; 45, a man in tunic and hood, lying on his side and clasping his hands ; 46, a man in girded tunic, with his head downwards, upholding the seat with his back and left hand ; 47, head of a lady with hair in a caul on each side, covered with a veil confined by an ornate fillet ; 48, a gentle-looking lion ; 49, a bat displayed ; 50, head of an angel, with amice round neck and expanded wings ; 51, a lion ; 52, two doves about to drink from a ewer standing in a basin (unfinished) ; 53, a squirrel with a collar round his neck, trying to escape from a monkey who holds him by a cord ; 54, a wood-pigeon feeding ; 55, a man riding on a lion, to whose buttocks he is applying a whip ; 56, a boar and a cat with cloven feet, walking in opposite directions ; 57, an eagle displayed (unfinished) ; 58, head and shoulders of a man who upholds the seat with his hands ; 59, a rabbit regardant ; 60, a two-legged beast regarding its tail, which is formed of three oak-leaves on one stem. *In the Library.*—61, a man in hood and loose tunic, kneeling on the ground and thrusting a spear down the throat of a dragon ; 62, a boy in gown, with long, wavy hair, lying on his side and drawing a thorn out of his left foot (of coarse late seventeenth-century work) ; 63, a dove or pigeon feeding her young ; 64, a sorrowful-looking king sitting cross-legged on a cushion between two rampant griffins, who are secured by straps buckled round their necks.

Glass in the Choir.—Over the high altar is a superb specimen of the Jesse window. It is so intricate, that at first nothing can be distinguished in the glow of jewelled colour but the twining branches of the vine, and a little time is needed to enter into the spirit of a window that is all the more enduring for not being very obvious. The following excellent description by Canon Church (in a sermon preached in the cathedral on May Day 1890) will make the legend easy to decipher :—

"In the central light are the foremost figures of the Bible story. At the base is the recumbent figure of Jesse with name inscribed, with head resting on hand as in meditation. From that figure, as from the vine stem, issues upward the leading shoot, bearing upon it the figures of the Virgin Mother crowned with ruby nimbus, and the Holy Child with gold nimbus, both under a golden canopy. Above, in line, is the Crucifixion. On either side, the waving tendrils of the vine shoots intertwine themselves in rings of light round figures of

those who prepared the way for the advent of the Word
Incarnate. On the lower tier, in line with Jesse, are, we
may believe, the ancestors of Jesse. Amminadab and Obed
are inscribed on two of the pedestals—others are nameless.
Stately figures they are in face and form, in flowing mantles of
green, and ruby and gold, like Arab chiefs, some with the
Arab head-covering such as is worn to-day—figures such as
some artist in the last crusading host might have seen and designed, so different from the conventional portraiture of Bible
characters.

"In the second tier are the Kings and Prophets chosen to
represent the heralds of the Babe of Bethlehem, the Word
Incarnate. Three kings—David with his 'immortal harp of
golden wires'; Solomon, with Temple model in his hand, in
robes of emerald, and ruby, and gold, are on either side of the
central Figures; and Jechonias, the link in the pedigree
between the royal David and the captive exile. Three Prophets
—Abraham, misplaced indeed in order of time, but most fitly
in place as 'the father of the faithful, unto whom and through
whom the gospel was before preached to the Gentiles' (Gal.
iii. 8); Hosea, and Daniel. All these are clad in the magnificence of Oriental drapery, the colours of each pair on either
side of the central light answering like to like. Some are
looking upward, some are pointing with outstretched hand
towards The Child, towards the Crucified One.

"There in central light in the mid-panel of the window is
the Virgin Mother and the Holy Child, The Child born in
Bethlehem the home of Jesse, not in David's royal Palace, the
flowering shoot of the stem of Jesse. Now from His throne
on His Mother's knee He looks out over the world and as
with outstretched arms to embrace. A ray of white light on
the Mother's head gives a natural halo of purity to Her 'the
highly favoured' 'with grace replete,' whom all generations
have called 'blessed,' as she looks down wondering on the
Holy Child.

"A subdued and sadder colour seems to veil the subject of
the highest panel in the central light. There is the green Cross
in the background, and upon it are affixed the attenuated arms
and the bent form of the Crucified—the head drooping on the
breast. On either side of the Cross stand, the sorrowing
Mother on the right, in attitude of calm resignation, very

different from the conventional garb of mourning, and the exaggerated expression of grief in so many paintings ; on the other hand St. John, in sadder colours and the gloom of grief. Again above, in two of the smaller six-cusped lights, are figures rising from the tomb, and in the two at the side are angels blowing trumpets calling to judgment. At the head and apex of the window are outstretched wings as of the Holy Spirit like the Dove brooding over the world re-created by the Word made Flesh, giving Himself for our redemption."

The clerestory windows contained a figure under a canopy in each of the lower lights. Four of these old windows remain. One light in the north-east window contains a St. George, thus described by Mr C. Winston (*Arch. Soc., Bristol vol.*) : " He is clad in a surcoat which reaches to the knee. He wears a helmet, avant and rerebras, shin-pieces and sollerets of plate, or rather cuir boulli ; the rest of his person is defended with mail, on his shoulders are aiglettes." In the next window are St. Egidias with very distended ears, and St. Gregory in a tiara. There are also two modern windows ; a glaring one by Wille-ment has St. Dunstan and St. Benignus, who were both abbots of Glastonbury and St. Honorius ; another, by Bell, has Augustine, Ambrose, and Athanasius.

The Aisles of the Choir are entered from the transepts by ogee arches, which have crockets and finials, and are flanked by a pair of pinnacles on either side. The aisles are of the same character as the choir itself, as they were vaulted when the choir vault was made, and new windows of the Decorated style were inserted in the western bays as well as in the newer part. There is a stone bench along the aisles on both sides, and on the north side some very fine specimens of Early English carving lie on the bench. The vaulting is lierned with four bosses at each intersection. The foliage of the third group of capitals on the north side consists of a single leaf which runs horizontally round the caps.

Two old wooden doors, with fine hinges, close the entrance to the presbytery on the north and south sides.

The body of Bishop Jocelin lies buried in the midst of the choir, where he was laid in the place of honour as a founder. Bishop Godwin relates that the tomb was " monstrously defaced " in his time, and all traces of the burying-place were lost until, in 1874, an ancient freestone coffin was found under the pavement in the midst of the choir. Its covering stone had been broken, and the bones within disturbed; but on its discovery the stone was renewed, and the inscription *Jocelinus de Welles, Ep.* 1242 cut on it.

The South-East Transept is the chapel of St. John the Evangelist, but it is mainly occupied by a stove, one of those characterised by Mr Freeman as "the most hideous stoves with which human perversity ever disfigured an ancient building." Odds and ends are also kept here, in accordance with the extraordinary idea, not yet quite extinct, that a chapel is a place where rubbish may be shot. There is, nevertheless, a decorated piscina in the east wall to remind one of its former purpose. Against the south wall is the tomb of the learned *Dean Gunthorpe* (1472-98), who built the present Deanery, and gave to the cathedral a silver image of our Lady, 158 oz. in weight. His initials occur on the panels, I. G. on a blue ground, and also his arms, which include guns, in allusion to his name. There are traces of colour, especially a strong light blue on the panels. Unless one has good nerves, it is advisable not to look at the window, which was given by the students of the Theological College under Canon Pindar, its first Principal. The middle of this unfortunate chapel is encumbered with a monument to *Dean Jenkyns* (*ob.* 1854), the ornamentation of which may be taken as marking the lowest point to which the debasement of Gothic design has descended. A row of tiles round it serves to make it more conspicuous, and its unhappy prominence is further secured by a low brass railing of unutterably bad workmanship. It was Dean Jenkyns who restored the choir, and Professor Freeman remarks that on his tomb "is written, with an unconscious sarcasm, *Multum ei debet ecclesia Wellensis*," words which, he slily points out, seem to be borrowed from Lucan's address to Nero, the destroyer of Rome, *Multum Roma tamen debet*, etc.

Monuments in the South Choir Aisle.—Besides two of the thirteenth-century effigies of earlier bishops, there are in this aisle two ancient monuments of great interest. In the second bay is the tomb of *Saint William Bytton* (1267-1274), a low slab of Purbeck marble, with the figure of a bearded and fully-vested bishop, in the act of benediction, cut upon it. This is the oldest incised slab in England; and it was at this tomb that the offerings were made which helped to finish the church. Godwin says that "many superstitious people (especially such as were troubled with the tooth-ake) were wont (even of late yeeres) to frequent much the place of his buriall, being without the North [a mistake for south] side of the Quier, where we see a Marble stone, having a pontificall image graven upon it."

It may have once been more raised than now, and four small plugged holes in the masonry of the wall opposite suggest the existence of some arrangement in connection with the devotions here. In the restoration of 1848 the tomb was discovered between the second and third piers of the south choir aisle. It is thus described by Mr J. R. Clayton, an eye-witness on the occasion :

"On the coffin being opened in the presence of Dean Jenkyns, it contained a skeleton laid out in perfect order, every bone in its right place ; an iron ring, and a small wooden pastoral staff in two fragments ; a leaden tablet, 10 in. by $3\frac{1}{3}$, with inscription most beautifully rendered in Lombardic characters.

> *Hic jacet Willelmus de Button secundus Bath-*
> *oniensis et Wellensis episcopus sepultus XII.*
> *die Decembris anno domini MCCLXXIIII."*

It was noted at the same time that "the teeth were absolutely perfect in number, shape, and order, and without a trace of decay, and hardly any discoloration." From this one would infer that the saint was famous in his lifetime for his beautiful teeth, and that it was for this reason that his aid came to be invoked after his death by those suffering from toothache. It is certainly curious that men now living should have discovered his teeth to be still in such perfect preservation. His con-temporaries would, no doubt, have called it a miracle.

A little farther east is the remarkable tomb of *Bishop Beckington*, surrounded by an exquisite iron screen of the same period. Its canopy formerly projected into the choir, being large enough to form a small chantry ; but, when the choir was so stupidly restored, the canopy was dragged from its place, and set up in St. Calixtus' chapel, where it still is (p. 99,) a hard-looking stone screen being built between the tomb and the choir in its stead. The tomb is divided into two parts, the arcade which forms the canopy of the lower effigy supporting the slab on which rests the figure of the bishop. The carving is very beautiful, and the delicately-wrought wings of the angels, which spread over the arches so as to fill the spandrels, are especially fine. Traces of colour are strong on the tomb, as they are on the canopy from which it has been divorced, so that one can form some little idea of what the whole must have been like in its first magnificence.

The effigy of the bishop rests upon it, the old and wrinkled face (best seen from within the choir) bearing deep traces of that active public life which did so much for the city and the church. Below, in strange contrast to the gorgeous vestments, which have still the remnants of the painted pattern on them, lies a corpse, almost a skeleton, in its open shroud. At first one's feeling is that of repulsion, but it is lessened when we remember that Beckington himself had the tomb made, and consecrated it before a vast concourse of people, saying mass for his own soul, for those of his parents, and of all the faithful departed in the January of 1452. Thus for thirteen years did this great and famous prelate live with his tomb standing as a witness to all that, under those sumptuous robes of office which we are told he wore at its consecration, he knew himself to be but as other men, and could wait humbly for his end.

A little farther east is a large and rather clumsy effigy of *Bishop Harewell* (*ob.* 1386), whose name and arms are suggested, in the playful fashion of the time, by two hares at his feet. Harewell is known to have been a portly man.

To the west of Beckington's monument an altar tomb in reddish alabaster has been placed in memory of *Lord Arthur Hervey*, the late bishop, with an effigy by Mr Brock. It may be hoped that it is the last of its kind, since there is little room for more tombs, and great need of other and more useful forms of memorial.

Bishop Drokensford's tomb, at the entrance to the south-east transept, is of unusual design, the ogee heads of its panels being through-cut from side to side. Only the bases remain of its canopy, which was taken down in 1758, as it was thought to be in danger of falling. There is a good deal of colour on the tomb; the chasuble is red with green lining, its orphreys are painted on the stone. The apparel is also painted on the alb, the orphreys and ornaments on the mitre, and a lozenge-shaped pattern on the cushion. Two shields are emblazoned over and over again on the spandrels, the ground being alternately red and green with white sprays of foliage ; the coat with four swans' heads, couped and addorsed, is Drokensford's. He was bishop when Dean Godelee's great works were going on, and he gave money towards building the central tower.

Monuments of the North Choir Aisle.—One of the Early English effigies, which were made probably by Bishop Jocelin, lies here, with a modern inscription, to *Bishop Giso*. There are four others, to *Æthelwyn*, *Leofric*, *Duduc*, and *Burwold*, all having the same characteristics, in the ambulatory chapels and opposite aisle. Graceful and solemn as they are, they seem rough in outline, as if they were carved by a hand used to calculating for the distant views of the west front, and almost weather-worn, by the side of the more highly-finished effigies in marble and alabaster which are near them. In the year 1848, when these monuments were set back and placed on their present ugly bases, they were found to contain boxes with bones therein, and leaden tablets with the name of each bishop inscribed upon them.

A different monument is that of *Ralph of Shrewsbury* (*ob.* 1363), whose marble effigy, scored by the names of long-departed vandals, affords a good example of the episcopal ornaments, the mitre, gloves, maniple, the apparel round the neck, and the vexillum round the crozier. The tomb formerly stood surrounded by a grating, in the midst of the presbytery, for Ralph was the "finisher" of the church. But it was afterwards moved, and, says Godwin, it "lost his grates by the way." At the entrance to the little transept is the tomb of *Dean Forrest* (*ob.* 1446), similar to that of Drokensford in the opposite aisle, but more mutilated. The canopy is gone, but fragments of it are in the undercroft of the chapter-house.

The North-East Transept is the chapel of St. John Baptist, and contains a Decorated piscina. On its east wall is a sculpture of the Ascension, which formerly was fixed in the east cloister above the I.H.S. in the fourth bay. St. Andrew with his cross may be noticed among the Apostles. There are traces of blue in the background, and of red in one of the cloaks. Most noticeable among its monuments is the handsome marble sarcophagus and effigy of *Bishop Creyghton*, who gave the lectern. The figure is vested in cope, mitre, and alb, a fact which is worth noting, as the bishop lived in the reign of Charles II. There is also an effigy of *John de Myddleton* or Milton, who, after being chancellor for a very short time, became a friar and died in 1337. The plain tomb of *Bishop Berkeley* (*ob.* 1581) bears a curious inscription, which assumes more than the character of its subject would seem to warrant : *Spiritvs, ervpto, salvvs, gilberte novembre, carcere principis en(c) æthere barkle, crepat. añ : dãt ista salutis.* Which may thus be translated, " Thy soul is safe, Gilbert Barkley, having broken from its prison in the beginning of November, it speaks from the sky. These words give the year of its safety." The words referred to are in the middle part of the tomb—

> *Vixi, videtis præmium :*
> *Lvxi, redux quieascibus.*
> 83 *Pro, captua gendo præsulis*
> *Septem per annos triplices*

The figures 83 at the side of *Vixi* and *Lvxi* suggested to Mr J. Parker that the letters stood also for figures thus—vi (6) xi (11) lv (55) xi (11), the total being 83, which was the age at which Berkeley died. The quatrain may be translated—

> " I have lived, you see my reward :
> I have shone, returning to my rest.
> Having held the office of bishop
> For seven times three years."

The east end of the north aisle forms a roomy chapel which is dedicated to St. Stephen, and contains a piscina of the same type as those in the neighbouring chapels. Its east window has five lights, and that in the side wall has three, with good reticulated tracery ; the principal mouldings are already assuming the large flat hollow form which was to become characteristic of the Perpendicular style. The chapel of St. Catherine on the south side corresponds to it exactly.

The Procession Path, or, to use the uglier and more accurate word, the Retro-choir, is a rectangular space between these chapels and the transepts, on the north and south, and the Lady Chapel and presbytery on the east and west. This space is vaulted ; and the vault is carried by four slender piers of Purbeck marble, with attached shafts, in the midst, by a group of Purbeck shafts on each of the two piers which lead into the Lady Chapel, and by the light blue Purbeck shafts of the eastern arches of the presbytery. As two of the middle piers (which are set diagonally from north-east to south-west, and from south-east to north-west) are in a line with the pier-arches of the choir, while the other two, though in a line with those of the Lady Chapel (which themselves project into the Path), are without those of the choir, a complicated system of vaulting and a charming arrangement of piers is the result. Indeed, this exquisite group of piers has never been surpassed, and nothing

Dawkes & Partridge, Photo.]
PROCESSION PATH AND LADY CHAPEL.

can be found that better illustrates the subtlety and extreme refinement of the last stages of Gothic architecture at their best. At whichever point one stands fresh beauty is apparent. It is merely a device for connecting Lady Chapel with choir, while leaving a wide path free for processions, yet what a gem of perfection has been drawn from the need! As one sits at the corner near the south wall of the Lady Chapel, one can best appreciate the range of vaulting, which, though it is doubled here, is of the same height as that of the aisles, running faithfully round to cover the ambulatory which encircles the choir, while on either side the pillars soar upward to the higher vault of the Lady Chapel and the yet higher ceiling of the choir. Opposite are the painted fragments of glass in the north choir aisle, seen through the arches of the presbytery, and the windows over the range of tabernacle work in the choir itself. On the left the south aisle can be seen stretching onwards, across the bright break of the transept, to the west end, and on the right are the gorgeous windows of the Lady Chapel. Everywhere the slender pillars stand, and the mouldings branch away from their rich capitals, each doing its appointed work, calculated and exact, in what would seem at first but a lavish profusion of marble shaft and moulded stone. Yet we can hardly now imagine what it all was like before the richly-decked altars were torn down, the painted windows knocked to fragments, the canopies, tombs, and images defaced or destroyed.

The vault is lierned with richly-carved bosses still warm with the marks of gilding; both on the bosses and the capitals the foliage is of the crumpled character suggestive of the oak-leaf.

Unlike the piers of the Lady Chapel, the bases here are of marble, though the plinths are of stone. Two grotesque heads, lower than the bosses, at the north and south-western angles, hold three ribs in their mouths, the ribs, which end there in seeming futility, being used to cover an awkward corner of the vaulting.

Glass in the Choir Aisles and Chapels.—A good deal of glass in a more or less fragmentary condition survives in the eastern portion of the church. It is fine work of the first half of the fourteenth century. In the south aisles there is good glass in all the upper lights; the third window has later glass in the lower lights, which bears the date 1607, and consists of coats of arms and a series of small square pictures of foreign type. The east window of St. Catherine's chapel is composed of fragments fitted together at random; in the upper lights of the south window are rather coarse heads of St. Aldhelm, St. Erkenwald, and other saints: two of them should be noticed for the early form of papal tiara. In the corresponding chapel of St. Stephen both the east and north windows are the same, the north window even containing a second head of St. Erkenwald; the other saints are inscribed—

"St. Stephanas Papa" (the Pope Stephen, who died 257),
"S. Blasii Epi" (St. Blaise), and "S. Marcellus Papa"; in the
topmost light of both windows is a small figure of Our Lord.

In the north aisle, the first window (counting from the east)
contains a St. Michael; the next a crucifix and a figure of St.
Mary Magdalen, with some sixteenth-century coats (including
the curious arms of Bishop Knight, p. 87) in the lower lights.
Similar coats are in the third window, which has a figure of
St. John Baptist. The fourth window contains modern glass
erected in honour of Bishop Ken (p. 157), as a memorial to
Dean Plumptre, who died in 1891. In the centre Ken is
represented in full pontifical vestments, below him angels are
supporting his arms impaled with those of the see; over his head
is the favourite superscription of his letters, "All glory be to God,"
and at his feet his rule of life "*Et tu quæris tibi grandia?
Noli quærere*" (Jer. xlv. 5). The left-hand panels represent St.
Paul teaching Timothy (because Ken wrote the "Manual for
Winchester Scholars," and the "Exposition of the Catechism"),
Christ's charge to St. Peter; the right panels represent St.
Paul before Agrippa and St. Peter in prison (because Ken was
one of the seven bishops imprisoned by James II.). The two
lower panels represent labourers going to their work singing
Benedicite, and a priest and choristers chanting *Nunc Dimittis*,
in allusion to Ken's morning and evening hymns.

The Lady Chapel was finished in 1326, before the
presbytery was added to the present choir, and thus it belongs
to the middle of the Decorated period. In plan it is octagonal,
the three western sides consisting of the three arches by
which it is opened to the rest of the church. It could, in
fact, stand perfectly well as a detached building like the Lady
Chapel at Gloucester, and doubtless it did so stand while the
presbytery was a-building; but its connection with the church
itself allows its apsidal west end to be cunningly combined
with the beautiful pillars which support the vault of the
ambulatory. The arrangement by which these three western
sides project into the ambulatory is more easy to see than to
describe; from the west side of the piers which support them
spring the vaulting ribs of the retro-choir, while on the east
side of the piers the shafts rise much higher up to carry the
loftier vault of the Lady Chapel. As the chapel is not a perfect
octagon like the chapter-house, but is elongated from east to

west, this vault was difficult to manage, and its lines are somewhat distorted in consequence. The vault springs from triple shafts between fine traceried windows of five lights, and its ribs meet in a boss containing a beautiful figure of our Lord seated on a throne with outstretched arms; the colour and gilding are well restored.

Professor Willis said that "the polygonal Lady Chapel and the vaulted work which connects it with the presbytery is a most original and unique piece of architecture, of pure and beautiful design." As to the first part of this sentence there can be no difference of opinion, and all will agree as to the fineness of the general effect of the chapel; yet there may well be two opinions as to the purity of the work. I confess that the following criticism (*Builder*, Aug. 1862) from a lecture of Mr E. W. Godwin seems to me to be not entirely without justification :—" With the single exception of the way in which the vaulting is managed, I look upon this Lady Chapel as no better than the other work of the same date. There is a weakness about the constant recurrence of the same form in the tracery of the windows; the lines of the vault are, in some cases, clumsy to a degree; and the capitals have lost their constructional character altogether. The growth and vitality, the change and joyfulness, so visible in the earlier caps, especially those with figures, are no longer to be seen. Leaves are now stuck on; or, at the best, wreathed round the bell of the capital; and so the *function* of the capital—the upbearing principle—is lost." So much for its defects. The peculiar excellence of the chapel is that it gives that apsidal ending to the church which adds so much to its beauty both within and without, and yet does not interfere with the square end of the presbytery.

The Lady Chapel has been fitted up for the use of the Theological College, and its furniture contrasts favourably with that of the choir. A litany desk, stalls, and credence-table in oak have recently been given, and a retable carved by Miss Neville; the altar cross, however, is too stunted for its position. The eagle lectern, in spite of its dark appearance, is modern, of Dean Goodenough's time. The doorway on the south side led to the old vestry, so wantonly destroyed in the present century: now that the chapel is in daily use the need of the vestry is much felt, and a cupboard in St. John's chapel has to serve for a makeshift. The gas-brackets are of later and more pleasant work than those elsewhere.

Mr Ferrey discovered fragments of a reredos at the east end of the chapel, and set them up as best he could to form the present reredos : the original arrangement seems to be lost, for some of the pedestals are on the level of the floor, while some of the niches at the top are cut in half. Mr Ferrey restored the whole chapel at the same time, and paved it with tiles.

Glass in Lady Chapel.—The large windows of this chapel are all filled with beautiful fourteenth-century glass, but alas! in a marred condition. The side windows contain fragments packed together anyhow. The eastern window was made up out of old pieces by Willement at Dean Goodenough's restoration, and its colour almost completely spoilt by modern insertions. The harm, however, is not irreparable, for the figures are almost entirely genuine, and the bad effect is mainly due to Willement's blue background. A careful examination would easily separate the new from the old, and it would be quite easy at the present day to remove the bad work and replace it by glass that would carry out the old harmony of colour. The lower lights are filled with two tiers of figures in canopies, David and other patriarchs in the upper tier, and the following well-chosen series in the lower :—The Madonna in the midst, on her right the Serpent and Eve, on her left the Brazen Serpent and Moses. The upper lights of this window contain angels bearing the instruments of the Passion, which are unspoilt, as are also the busts of patriarchs in the north-east window, and of bishops in that on the south-east. Three of the topmost lights contain emblems of the Evangelists, the fourth is lost. One inscription remains, *Ista capella constructa est* . . . but the date is gone.

A tall and light monument stands between the Lady Chapel and St. Catherine's ; its crocketed finials, filled with tracery, rise almost to the ceiling. The canopy is open at the sides and western end, but the eastern end forms a niche ; this part has been restored in colour and gilding, it is powdered with *fleurs-de-lys*, and bears a shield containing the *Agnus Dei*. No other part shows any trace of colour. The base is much higher than that of an ordinary tomb, and the canopy seems to have been somewhat altered at Ferrey's restoration.

The spot where the altar of St. Catherine and All Virgins

stood is now "Sacred to the memory of John Phelips Of Montacute in this county esquire. Descended from a line of ancestors, Whose names for two centuries and a half abound in the annals of the county, He succeeded at an early age to the paternal estates, And sustained the wonted hospitality of his house. He soon became a most active and intelligent magistrate," etc., etc.

The Chapter-House Staircase is entered by the door-way in the eastern aisle of the north transept. There are few things in English architecture that can be compared with it for strange impressive beauty; the staircase goes upward for eighteen steps and then part of it sweeps off to the chapter-house on the right, while the other part goes on and up till it reaches the chain-bridge; thus the steps lie, worn here and there by the tread of many feet, like fallen leaves, the last of them lost in the brighter light of the bridge. Here one is still almost within the cathedral, and yet the carts are passing under-neath, and their rattle mixes with the sound of the organ within.

The date of the staircase is clearly somewhere between that of the chapter-house and that of the church itself. It is later than the church, for it is built up against the transept buttresses, and it contains some of the best examples of simple geometrical tracery, while there are nothing but lancet windows in the church of Reginald and Jocelin. But the simple geometrical tracery of its two four-light windows prove that it was finished before the chapter-house was begun. The arches of these windows are rampant, to follow the level of the stairs; their beautiful circular tracery is massive, deeply-moulded, and filled with remnants of rich glass; their shafts of blue lias have naturalistic capitals which are in striking contrast both to the Early English carving in the church and the full Decorated of the chapter-house itself. Below the windows is a stone bench rising in steps with a foot-pace of similar construction; this arrangement adds much to the effect of the staircase, though it is marred by a modern hand-rail.

Before the Chain Gate was made, the vestibule ended with a graceful window of four lights similar to those at the side. The upper part of the window remains, but the lower part is occupied by a Perpendicular doorway, and the whole now forms a screen which, by breaking the light, adds considerably to the charm of the staircase. Through this doorway, where

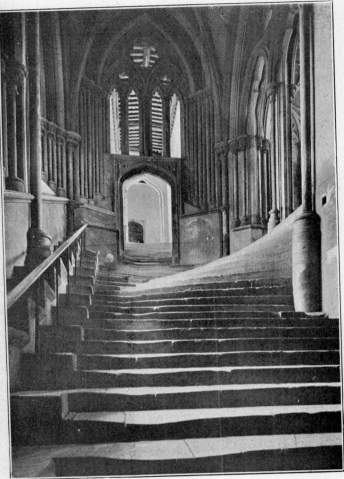

STEPS OF CHAPTER-HOUSE VESTIBULE AND PASSAGE OVER
CHAIN GATE.

they are cut away to allow the door to open, the steps continue for two stages, but in a narrower flight. Here the windows are Perpendicular, and the vaulted ceiling has given place to a wooden roof, for this is the Chain Gate, as light and pretty within as without. It was only an after-thought, a matter of convenience, thus to connect the chapter-house with the Vicars' Close, and the screen that now breaks the light had for a century and a half been the outside window, just as the blocked window of the transept had been the outer light for the fifty years before the staircase itself was thought of. It was just a practical matter-of-fact device; but what magnificent utilitarianism, what an inspired after-thought!

The main gallery of the Chain Gate is shut off by a door which, if it were kept open, would make the prospect even more beautiful than it is. Two corbels which support the vaulting-shafts of the lower staircase should be noticed; they both represent figures thrusting their staves into the mouth of a dragon, but that on the east (wearing a hood and a leathern girdle round his surcoat) is as vigorous in action as the figure on the west side is feeble. A small barred opening in the top of the east wall lights a curious little chamber, which is reached from the staircase that leads to the roof.

The Chapter-House is entered by a double-arched doorway, the small vault between the arches having an odd boss composed of four bearded heads. There are marks in the wall which lead one to think that the doors were hung in a wooden screen under this vault. The old doors are now used in the house of the Principal of the College, where they were identified by Canon Church. They have little slits in them, through which those in the chapter-house could speak with those without, who no doubt waited for admittance on the stepped stone bench of the staircase. Grooves in the two inner shafts of the doorway seem to have been made for the insertion of some light screen, by which the entrance was divided into two passages for ingress and egress. The absence of doors certainly adds to the rather cold unfurnished appearance of the chapter-house in its present condition.

The room itself ("a glorious development of window and vault" it has been called) is one of the best examples of that type of chapter-house which belongs mainly to the thirteenth century, and is a peculiar glory of English architecture. Of

octagonal plan, its vaulting ribs branch out from sixteen
Purbeck shafts which cluster round the central pillar, typifying
the diocesan church with all its members gathered round its

Dawkes & Partridge, Photo.]
CHAPTER-HOUSE—DOORWAY.

common father, the bishop. Each of the eight sides of the
room is occupied by a window of four lights, with graceful
tracery of an advanced geometrical type. These windows,
which are among the finest examples of the period, have no

shafts, but their arch mouldings are enriched with a continuous series of the ball-flower ornament. Most of the old glass, in which ruby and white are the predominant colours, remains in the upper lights.

Under the windows runs an arcade which forms fifty-one stalls, separated into groups of seven by the blue lias vaulting-shafts at the angles, but in the side which is occupied by the

Dawkes & Partridge, Photo.]
CHAPTER-HOUSE—INTERIOR.

doorway there are only two stalls, one on either side of the entrance. Two rows of stone benches are under the stalls, and there is a bench of Purbeck round the base of the central pier. The arcade strikes one as too shallow : its canopies, which rest on blue lias shafts, are ornamented with feathering, crockets, finials, and an interesting series of small heads. Some of the heads wear crowns, mitres, hoods, and square caps ; others are grotesque, though I cannot detect the " jesters " to which some writers refer. Some of the heads have the same formal twist in the hair as those of the large corbels in the nave (p. 81). The heads on the side opposite the door are all (with the exception of one modern head in plaster) covered with the early form of papal tiara, a conical hat with a crown round its rim. On this side, in the middle stall, is the bishop's seat, and here are traces of colour; the little heads are still pretty with pink cheeks and painted eyes and hair, and above the canopy the saltire of St. Andrew is discernible.

Thus the bishop still retained, at least in theory, the head-ship of the chapter. The dean sat on one side of him, the precentor on the other, and the rest in due order from the archdeacons and officers down to those in minor orders. Even the boys of the school were admitted to part of the meetings, and they stood on the floor round a desk which was in front of the chief pastor. "There every morning," says Canon Church (*Chapters in Hist. of Wells*, p. 333), "after the prayers of the third hour and the morning mass, the chapter of the whole body was held for the daily lection and commemoration of brethren departed, for maintaining discipline, hearing com-plaints, passing judgment, inflicting punishment; for ordering the services of the day and of the week—for sitting in council and drawing up statutes."

Beautiful as is the general effect of the chapter-house, it must be admitted that its detail is inferior to that of the stair-case, which is just one stage earlier in the development of architecture. Nor can its capitals be compared for a moment with those in the nave; the lighter form of structure doubtless calls for a lighter cap, but these are distinctly untidy in their decoration. The crockets are very near having that wholesale look which has caused nineteenth-century architects to make so much of this easily debased ornament. The arrangement, too, by which the fine doorway rises into a window of unmodified pattern seems a rather awkward compromise, especially as the line of the staircase roof cuts slantwise across the lights. One cannot help thinking that an earlier architect would have departed from his uniform pattern at this point, and have inserted a window or arcade better adapted to the position, with the addition, perhaps, of sculpture in the vacant space.

Between the roof and the vault there is a curious chamber which reminds one of the crater of a volcano, and the impression is increased by the sponge-like stone, which has some resemblance to tufa. The open arcade under the roof has served to keep the woodwork in remarkably sound condition.

Dawkes & Partridge, Photo.]
CHAPTER-HOUSE—VAULT.

The Undercroft.—Much of the external beauty of the chapter-house, as well as the charm of its staircase, is due to its unusual height above the ground. It rests upon a vaulted chamber or undercroft, which is popularly called the crypt,

though that term is not very accurate, as the chamber is not
sunk underground, but stands almost on a level with the floor
of the church. The innumerable springs in the soil of Wells
do not, indeed, admit of a subterranean building. The undercroft was finished before the chapter-house staircase was begun;
perhaps its walls were built at the end of Jocelin's episcopate;
at any rate it was finished by 1286, and represents the last
development of the Early English style. It was used as the

CHAPTER-HOUSE—UNDERCROFT.

treasury, where the vestments, ornaments, registers, and other
precious things, both of the bishop and chapter, were kept,
and, to increase the security of its massive walls, the sacristan
had to sleep within them every night.

It is reached by a dimly-lit, impressive passage, which is
entered from the north choir aisle through a doorway with
deeply-sunk mouldings and carved capitals. Two heads, slant-
ing inwards in a rather awkward manner, support the curious
pediment-shaped canopy over the doorway. At the commence-

ment of this fine passage, just within the doorway, is a small
vault supported on extremely odd corbels, as if the mason had
taken advantage of the obscurity to wanton with his craft.
One is a large head with enormous cheeks, apparently suffering
from acute neuralgia; a handkerchief, under which a few
comically-stiff curls escape, covers the head and is tied under
the chin; another represents two dragons biting each other,
with a head upside down beneath them; another, which re-

CHAPTER-HOUSE—UNDERCROFT.

minds one of the worst eccentricities of modern crockery, is
formed by a hand holding a foliated capital. I suppose that
the head with swollen cheeks is really another testimony to St.
William Bytton's power over the toothache. The undercroft
itself was finished before 1286, perhaps some time before; but
the more advanced sculpture of the passage looks as if that
part were built in the "toothache" period—that is to say, some
ten years or so after Bytton's death in 1274.

Certainly the bosses of the vault in the passage beyond the

doorway are of a character that suggests the transition to Decorated which was in progress at this time. They are elaborate, and, with one exception, through-carved. The first from the door represents a head, the next an *Agnus Dei*, the next two grotesque heads joined together, then apparently the Serpent tempting Eve, then an ox, dragons, two small grinning heads, with animals apparently biting them on one side. The corbels are carved into heads, some crowned, others reversed with the shaft in their mouths. On the right-hand side, as one enters the undercroft, a pretty stone lantern projects from the wall; of the little mullions which form its face, one is set far enough from the wall to admit of the insertion of a lamp.

Two heavy wooden doors at the entrance leave no doubt as to the purpose for which the undercroft was built. The outer door is the most massive; it is studded with nails, and has two great bolts and a huge lock : on the outer side a kind of escutcheon is formed round the keyhole by a heart-shaped piece of iron, surmounted by a cross; on the same side there is an iron bar, and the hook to hold it across the doorway. A deep hole has been worn in the pavement by the feet of those who pulled open the door. The inner door is lighter, and ornamented with beautiful elaborate hinges : on this side are deep sockets in the wall, into which the inner bars were run.

In the undercroft itself the walls are impregnably thick, the windows narrow, with wide splays. The vaulting, somewhat later in style than the walls, is an admirable piece of construction, well-fitted to bear the weight of the lofty chamber above. It is also remarkable, Professor Willis points out, for the way in which the arches are disposed without the introduction of ribs. From the round shafts which are grouped about the octagonal pier in the centre spring the vaulting ribs, the extremities of which rest upon eight round pillars ; and another set of vaulting ribs spans the space between these pillars and the eight walls, where they rest upon twelve shafts between the lancet windows. Could anything be more simple and secure in construction, and more varied in effect ?

Here, on one of the capitals and on a moulding near the door, we meet with the dog-tooth moulding usually so characteristic of the Early English style. The piscina in the doorway should be noticed for its carving of a dog gnawing a bone.

A large aumbry is formed by a recess in the thickness of the wall.   The parapeted structure opposite is a modern coal-hole, for which some other place might surely be found.

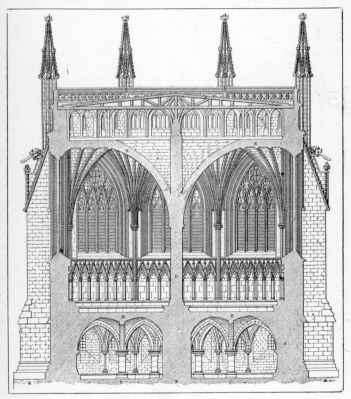

SECTION OF CHAPTER-HOUSE.

There are several stone coffins in the undercroft, and a good many fragments of carved stone, some of which are very fine. Here also is a cope-chest of the usual shape, which allows the copes to be put away with only one fold.   Near it there is a large oblong chest covered with iron bands. An iron door which is also kept here is thus described by Mr H. Longden (*Archæological Journal*, 1890, p. 132): "It is made of slabs of iron nailed to an oak frame-work, and liberally braced across with hinges and diagonal cross-straps, stiffening the door in the best way known at the time. This is not an iron-plated door, but an iron door; it is, in fact, a 'safe' door of the time, and is an uncommon instance. It must be remembered that the slabs of which this door is formed were all beaten out of lumps of iron, and that iron was not then made, as now, in plates, bars, or rods, but . . . The lump of iron had to be heated and drawn out on the anvil at a great expenditure of time and labour. Much of the charm of old work arises from the irregularity of the shapes, never quite round, or square, or flat, which the iron took, and we miss this in the neat and mechanically-finished work of the present time."

CHAPTER IV.

HISTORY OF THE DIOCESE.

LEGEND, which in every ancient city is raised to the dignity of an article of faith, places the origin of Wells diocese in the remote past; and the visitor is required to believe that Ina, King of Wessex, the first great West Saxon lawgiver, the ruler who finally established the English supremacy in the south-west, was also the founder of the see of Wells. He is said to have planted a bishopric at Congresbury, and in 721 to have removed the see to Wells with the help of Daniel, the last British bishop. The story, however, rests upon no good foundation.

Before the middle of the seventh century the heathen invaders were converted by St Birinus, and by the time of Ina Wessex was divided into the dioceses of Winchester and Sherborne, the latter including Somerset, Dorset, and part of Wiltshire. This was all that Ina did towards establishing the diocese of Wells; and it did not go very far, for the special boast of the diocese is that it consists of one county, Somerset, and of nothing else. And so it is that the honour of possessing Ealdhelm, the first bishop of Sherborne, who tramped about, an open-air preacher, in his diocese, belongs to Salisbury and not to Wells; although Doulting, where Ealdhelm fell sick and died sitting in the little wooden village church, is the very place whence afterwards the stone was quarried for the building of Wells Cathedral.

It was under that great warrior, Edward the Elder, that the diocese of Sherborne was divided, and the Sumorsaetas received a bishop of their own, whose stool was placed in the church of St. Andrew at Wells.

It is quite probable that the above tradition grew around Ina's name owing to his having really established a church with a body of priests attached to it; since we find in a charter of Cynewulf, dated 766, a mention of "the minister near the great spring at Wells for the better service of God in the church of St. Andrew." This charter is probably spurious, but it may for all that enshrine an historical fact, especially as it does not pretend to the existence of a bishopric. If this be the case, then Edward, who wanted a fairly central church for a diocese which had no important town, must have found Wells very convenient for his purpose. For while Glastonbury, besides being in those days an island, had an abbot of its own, this little body of secular priests would be ready to receive the

SPECIMENS OF CAPITALS.

bishop as their chief, and to become his chapter. At all events, the year 909 saw Wells with a bishop of its own.

Aethelhelm or **Athelm,** *Bishop of Somerset, or Wells* (909-914), a monk of Glastonbury according to tradition, was the first Somersetshire bishop; he is said to have been an uncle of St. Dunstan: he was made Archbishop of Canterbury in 914.

It will be convenient to weave the history of the foundation of Wells with that of the bishops. So here, at the outset, the reader must bear in mind that from the beginning the cathedral church was served by "secular" clergy, by priests, that is, who were bound by no vows other than those of their ordination,

who did not live a community life, but had each his own
house, and generally at this time his own wife and family.
Wells Cathedral was not " built by the monks," and its chapter
was never composed of monks ; though some of the bishops
belonged to religious orders, it kept up a pretty constant rivalry
with the " regular " clergy of Glastonbury and Bath. It belongs
in fact, to the cathedrals of the old foundation, whose con-
stitutions were not changed at the Reformation ; and its chapter
has continued in unbroken succession, from the days when

SPECIMENS OF CAPITALS.

Aethelhelm first presided over his little body of clergy in the
church of St. Andrew, down to our own time. But at first that
chapter was informal enough, nor was it finally incorporated
and officered till the time of Bishop Robert in the twelfth
century. The number of canons does not seem to have been
fixed, though in the next century we hear of there being only
four or five.

The next five bishops are all little more than names to us.
Wulfhelm succeeded Aethelhelm in 914 : also translated to
Canterbury ; **Aelfheah** (923), **Wulfhelm** (938), **Brithhelm**
(956-973), and **Cyneward** (973-975).

Sigegar (975-977), a pupil of St. Dunstan, and abbot

of Glastonbury, was succeeded, or perhaps supplanted, by
Aelfwine, in 997-999.

Aethelstan, or **Lyfing**; translated to Canterbury 1013.

Aethelwine and **Brihtwine** shared the episcopate, either
as rivals or coadjutors. Brihtwine was last in possession.
Merewit, also called Brihtwine, succeeded in 1026.

Duduc (1033-1060), a German Saxon. Cnut had given
him the estates of Congresbury and Banwell, which he left to
the church of Wells; but Harold took possession of them.

Gisa (1060-1088), a Belgian from Lorraine, found his see
in a sad condition: the church was mean, its revenues small,
and its four or five canons were forced, he says, to beg their
bread. He at once set to work to increase the revenues; and
from Edward the Confessor, from his queen, Edith, then from
Harold, and afterwards from William the Conqueror, he
obtained various estates for the support of his canons.

He also changed the way of living of the canons, and built
a cloister, dormitory, and refectory, thereby forcing them
to live a common life, much as if they were monks—an un-
popular innovation which was supported by the appointment in
the foreign fashion of a provost to be chief officer, the canons
choosing for this post one Isaac of Wells.

John de Villula, *Bishop of Bath* (1088-1122), a rich
physician of Tours. He put an end to the semi-monastic
discipline of Gisa by pulling down his community buildings
and erecting a private house of his own on the site. And he
removed the see of Somersetshire from Wells to the Abbey of
Bath.

Godfrey (1123-1135).

Robert of Lewes (1136-1166), the second founder of the
cathedral; he made the constitution of the chapter, he rebuilt
the old Saxon church, and he started Wells as a borough by
the grant of its first charter of freedom. Of a Fleming family,
though born in England, he was a monk from the Cluniac
house of St. Pancras at Lewes; and to another and more
famous Cluniac monk, Bishop Henry of Winchester, King
Stephen's brother, he owed his advancement. In the very
year of his consecration he began the recovery of Wells from
the low estate in which John de Villula and his rapacious
relatives had left it. He restored their property to the canons,
and, in order to secure it, he divided it off from the property

of the see by a charter of incorporation. He assisted at Henry II.'s coronation in 1154, and at the consecration of Thomas à Becket in 1162.

Bishop Robert arranged the quarrel with Bath by settling that Bath should take precedence of Wells, but that the bishop should have his throne in both churches, and be elected by the two chapters conjointly.

By the charter which incorporated the chapter of Wells, Robert also settled portions of the estate, or prebends, on the twenty-two canons, and founded the offices of dean, precentor, chancellor, treasurer, sub-dean, provost, and sub-chanter, all of which, except the two last, still exist.

After an interval of eight years, **Reginald de Bohun** or **Fitz-Jocelin**, the Archdeacon of Sarum, was consecrated Bishop of Bath (1174-1191). Immediately afterwards he induced the monk who was soon to become famous as St. Hugh of Lincoln, to leave the Grande Chartreuse, and to come to England as prior of the first English charter-house. He built the greater part of the present nave transepts and choir ; for this end he made large gifts to the fabric fund, and collected gifts from others. He also extended the privileges of the town, and increased both the endowment and the number of the prebends.

Savaric, *Bishop of Bath and Glastonbury* (1192-1205), a relation of the Emperor Henry VI. In 1191 he started with Richard I. for the Holy Land. At Messina, though not yet in priest's orders, he obtained private letters from the king sanctioning his appointment to any bishopric to which he might be elected. Bishop Reginald was a kinsman of his, and, on his election to Canterbury, he obtained the vote of the convent of Bath for Savaric. The Justiciar gave at once the royal sanction, in spite of the protests of the canons of Wells, who had not been consulted. Savaric had meanwhile wisely established himself at Rome, and was able to obtain the Pope's consent. He was consecrated priest one day and bishop the next, but he still remained abroad.

Savaric, supported by the authority of King John, broke into Glastonbury with soldiers, starved and beat the monks, and, with great violence, established himself in possession.

His biography was compressed in a clever epigram :—

> " *Hospes erat mundo per mundum semper eundo,*
> *Sic suprema dies fit sibi prima quies,*"

admirably translated by Canon Bernard :

> " Through the world travelling, all the world's guest,
> His last day of life was his first day of rest."

Yet he was the first to institute the daily mass of Our Lady, as well as that for the faithful departed, in Wells Cathedral.

Jocelin Troteman de Welles, *Bishop of Bath and Glastonbury*, and after 1219 *Bishop of Bath* (1206-1242), is, after Ken, the most famous of Wells worthies. He came from a local stock, and spent all his time and money on the cathedral church, first as canon, then as bishop for thirty-six years. In 1208, when Pope Innocent III. laid England under an interdict, the bishop published it in his own diocese, and then fled the country, leaving his estates to be seized by John. On John's submission to the Pope in 1213, he returned, and two years later stood by Stephen Langton at Runnymede, putting his name as Bishop of Bath and Glastonbury to *Magna Charta*. When John was dead it was Jocelin who administered the oath to Henry III. at his coronation.

In 1219 Jocelin made terms with Glastonbury, which Savaric had seized, giving up the abbacy and the title in return for four manors. He founded a hospital, re-endowed the Lady mass which Savaric had instituted, increased the number of prebends (the estates, that is, which each maintained a canon) from thirty-five to fifty, provided houses for the canons, and a regular endowment for the vicars-choral, started a grammar school in addition to the choristers' school, and enclosed the bishop's park. But most of all is he famous for having rebuilt the church which Savaric's vagaries had let fall into dilapidation, and for having added to it the noble west front. So extensive were his repairs that in 1239 a reconsecration was necessary; and three years later he died, "God," says old Fuller, "to square his great undertakings, giving him a long life to his large heart." He was buried in the midst of the choir as a founder of the church; and as this interment marked out Wells as the chief church in the diocese, the monks of Bath were not told of his death till after he had been buried.

Roger, *first Bishop of Bath and Wells* (1244-1247). On Jocelin's death in 1242, the monks of Bath made a last effort to recover the supremacy which had drifted from them. Contrary to the agreement which had been made, they pushed through their own candidate, Roger, without consulting with the Wells chapter, and snatched the regal sanction and papal confirmation for their nominee before the chapter of Wells could make a move. At last, the Pope, after much litigation, decreed that, in order to avoid any further vacancy, Roger's election should be confirmed, but that henceforth the chapter of Wells should have an equal voice in the election of the bishop, who was to use the title of Bath and Wells. Roger was buried in his old abbey of Bath; he was, however, the last bishop to be there interred. The words of Peter Heylin are henceforward true of the see :—"The diocese of Bath and Wells, though it hath a double name, is one single bishopric. The bishop's seat was originally at Wells, where it still continues. The style of Bath came in but upon the bye."

William Button or **Bytton** (1248-1264).

Walter Giffard (1265-1266), a statesman-bishop, took the king's side, and, after the victory of Evesham, was rewarded with the chancellorship and the archbishopric of York.

William Bytton (the Saint) (1267-1274). When Robert of Kilwardy, provincial of the Dominicans, was made archbishop, he chose Bytton, on account of his saintliness, to consecrate him; and so great was the impression made by his holy life that he became the object of popular canonisation at his death. Miracles were worked at his tomb, and crowds flocked to it with offerings, especially such as were afflicted with toothache.

Robert Burnell (1275-1292), the greatest lawyer of his day, chancellor of Edward I.; built the hall of the episcopal palace

William of March or **de Marchia** (1293-1302), had been treasurer in 1290. Two unsuccessful efforts were made to obtain his canonisation.

Walter de Haselshaw (1302-1308), successively canon, dean, and bishop.

Under **John of Drokensford** (1309-1329) the chapter

obtained a strong confirmation of their rights as the result of a violent quarrel with the bishop, who had claimed the power of visiting the churches under capitular jurisdiction.

Ralph of Shrewsbury (1329-1363), Chancellor of Oxford, put the finishing stroke to the constitution of the cathedral by founding the College of Vicars. He was a great supporter of the friars, and left them a third of his property. Among his good deeds he disafforested the royal hunting ground of Mendip, and thus did great service to the people, "beef," as Fuller has it, "being better pleasing to the husbandman's palate than venison." At his death he was buried in the place of honour before the high altar, for it was under him that the last great building operations in the church of Wells were completed.

John Barnet (1363-66), translated from Worcester, was soon again moved to Ely. After **John Harewell** (1367-86), who helped to build the south-west tower, and **Walter Skirlaw** (1386-88), **Ralph Erghum** (1388-1400) was translated from Salisbury, and founded at Wells the much-needed college for the fourteen chantry priests, which was destroyed under Edward VI., and of which the memory is preserved in "College Lane." There were now, therefore, three distinct corporations at Wells—the Chapter, the College of Vicars, and the College of Chantry Priests. **Henry Bowett** (1401-1407) was promoted to York.

Nicholas Bubwith (1407-1424) is remembered by the almshouses at Wells which he endowed, by his provision for building the north-west tower, and by his chantry chapel. There was at this time another hospital called the Priory, which has now disappeared. He was one of the English envoys at the Council of Constance. Mandates were sent him by the archbishop for the prosecution of the Lollards, but there is no record of any proceedings having been taken, till **John Stafford** (1425-43) had succeeded him, when one William Curayn was compelled to abjure and receive absolution for some very reasonable heresies. Stafford was translated to Canterbury.

Thomas Beckington, or Bekynton (1443-65), was first tutor, then private secretary to Henry VI., and Keeper of the Privy Seal. His many works at Wells are noticed in our other chapters; in his will he states that he spent 6000 marks in repairing and adorning his palaces.   After his death, the mayor and corporation showed their gratitude by going annually to his tomb (p. 125) to pray for his soul.

Robert Stillington (1466-91) was a minister of Edward IV., and one of Richard III.'s supporters.   Accused in 1487 of helping Lambert Simnel, he was imprisoned at Windsor for the rest of his life.   **Richard Fox** (1492-94), Keeper of the Privy Seal, translated to Durham.   **Oliver King** (1495-1503), Chief Secretary of Henry VII.   A dream moved Bishop Oliver in 1500, to rebuild Bath abbey in the debased Perpendicular style with which we are now familiar.

The celebrated **Adrian de Castello** (1504-1518) obtained first Hereford and then Wells, as a reward for political services. As he never visited his diocese, his affairs were managed by another famous man, Polydore Vergil, who was archdeacon, and furnished the choir of Wells with hangings, "flourished," says Fuller, "with the laurel tree," and bearing an inscription, *Sunt Polydori munera Vergilii*.   Adrian, who was born of humble parents at Cornuto in Tuscany, had been made a cardinal in 1503 by the infamous Pope Alexander VI., and both his archdeacon and himself are prominent figures in Italian history of the period.

Cardinal Wolsey (1518-23) was appointed to the see, which he held together with the archbishopric of York ; he was therefore Bishop of Bath and Wells only in name, and was soon put in the enjoyment of the richer sees successively of Durham and Winchester.   He was followed by **John Clerk** (1523-41) and **William Knight** (1541-47).   The abbey of Bath was now suppressed, so that the bishop's seat was now at Wells alone, and (excepting that the style " Bath and Wells " remained) the see was restored to its original condition before John de Villulâ migrated to Bath.

William Barlow (1549-54) was translated from St. David's without even the form of a *conge d'elire*.   In return for this and certain money payments he made over a large portion of the episcopal property to the greedy Duke of Somerset ; he also secured the episcopal manor of Wookey for his own family. The other cathedral estates were similarly treated.   Barlow fled at the accession of Mary, but was caught and imprisoned in 1554.   He had in Henry's time recanted some Lollard tracts which he had written, and now under Mary he recanted once more. On the accession of Elizabeth, he (p. 81) accepted the poorer see of Chichester.

Gilbert Bourne (1554-59) had been Bonner's chaplain. At Elizabeth's accession he was deprived and imprisoned in the Tower. After 1562 he was kept in nominal custody, and died in 1569.

Gilbert Berkeley (1560-1581) succeeded him. **Thomas Godwin** (1584-90), the historian of Wells, succeeded Berkeley.

Another three years' vacancy was followed by the appointment of **John Still** (1593-1607). He and his successors, **James Montague** (1608-16), translated to Winchester, **Arthur Lake** (1616-26), a wise man and "most blessed saint," were mostly occupied in the fight with Puritanism. **William Laud** was bishop here for two years (1626-28), but his history belongs to London and Canterbury, whither he was translated. **Leonard Mawe** (1628-29), **Walter Curll** (1629-32), translated to Winchester, and **William Piers** (1632-70) followed. The latter, who put down the Puritan "lectures," and ordered all the altars in his diocese to be set against the east wall and railed in, lived to see all his work undone and then restored again at the accession of Charles II. **Robert Creyghton** (1670-72), who had been dean, succeeded him. He was a great musician (p. 113), and his gifts of ornaments to the cathedral have been already mentioned. **Peter Mews** (1673-1684) was translated to Winchester.

Thomas Ken (1685-90), the best and most famous of all the Somerset bishops, has left so great a name in the see, and figured in so many stirring events, that one can hardly believe that he was only given five years in which to use his influence upon history. Before he was made bishop, however, he had already given proof of that quiet courage which was more than once to thwart the will of princes. In 1679 he went to the Hague as chaplain to Mary, the wife of William of Orange. Here he expressed himself "horribly unsatisfied" with William's unkindness to his wife, and he incurred the Prince's anger by persuading Count Zulestein to marry a lady whom he had seduced. Soon after, when he was living at Winchester, he refused to allow the royal harbinger to use his prebendal house for the lodging of Nell Gwynn, on the occasion of Charles II.'s visit there in 1683. Charles, with characteristic generosity, thought all the more highly of him, and when he was told of

Bishop Mew's death, he said no one should have the see but "the little black fellow who refused his lodging to poor Nelly." Before the year was over, Charles was on his death-bed, and summoned Ken to his side. The bishop persuaded the king to send the Duchess of Portsmouth from the room and to call in the Queen. He then absolved him, although Charles would not receive the communion.

After the Monmouth rebellion (p. 17) he, with the Bishop of Ely, was sent to tell the Duke of his fate; he remained with the wretched man all through the night before his execution, and accompanied him on the scaffold. He then returned to his see, used all his influence on behalf of the unhappy peasants, and by his personal intervention, saved a hundred prisoners from death. He strongly opposed the Romanising policy of James II., and preached several sermons which had a large share in the formation of public opinion. He was one of the seven bishops who were committed to the Tower for petitioning the king against the order to the clergy to read the second Declaration of Indulgence. The incidents of that wonderful trial are familiar to all Englishmen, and it is notable that one of the richest dissenters in the city begged to have the special honour of giving security for the high church bishop of Bath and Wells.

But when the revolution came, Ken was found among those who were called non-jurors, because they regarded their oath of allegiance to James as still binding. He was consequently, in 1690, deprived of his see. He made a public protest in the cathedral against his deprivation, and continued to sign himself *T. Bath and Wells*, but he had to live in retirement, and with an income of only £20 a year. He died in 1710, and was buried in Frome Church at sunrise, in allusion to his morning hymn ("Awake, my soul, and with the sun"), and to his habit of rising with the sun.

Ken was in every way a great saint, and, like all the saints, he was distinguished by his love for the poor, and his care for their education. Among his customs it is recorded that he used to have twelve poor men to dine with him on Sundays, and that he was wont to go afoot in London when the other bishops rode in their coaches. He wrote many books, among them his "Manual of Prayers for the Use of Winchester Scholars." "His elaborate works," says Macaulay, "have long been forgotten; but his morning and evening hymns are still repeated daily in thousands of dwellings."

Richard Kidder (1691-1703) became bishop on the deprivation of Ken, Dr Beveridge having declined the offer of a see, the rightful ruler of which had been unjustly removed. Kidder did not, however, long enjoy his usurped position; for, on the night of November 26th, 1703, a great storm—the same that destroyed Winstanley in his lighthouse on the Eddystone—blew down a stack of chimneys in the palace, and thus killed both the bishop and his wife as they lay abed.

George Hooper (1704-27), an old friend of Ken, was next offered the see, but he urged the reinstatement of the rightful pastor. Queen Anne offered to restore Ken to his bishopric, but he importuned Hooper to accept, and from that time ceased to sign himself by his diocesan title. Hooper had preceded Ken, in 1677, as Princess Mary's spiritual adviser at the Hague, where he had won her back to the services of the church, and he had also been with Ken at Monmouth's execution. Almost as lovable and holy, he was more learned than his friend.

Hooper was succeeded by **John Wynne** (1727-43), **Edward Willes** (1743-73), and **Charles Moss** (1774-1802); all three were typical eighteenth-century prelates, rich and mostly non-resident.

Richard Beadon (1802-24), was translated from Gloucester.

George Henry Law (1824-45), a son of the Bishop of Carlisle, and brother of Lord Chief-Justice Ellenborough, was translated from Chester, and is said to have been an active prelate till his latter years. Hon. **Richard Bagot** (1845-54) came to Wells as a place of retirement after the worries which he had gone through, as Bishop of Oxford, during the Tractarian movement.

Robert John, Lord Auckland, was translated from Sodor and Man in 1854. At his death in 1869, he was succeeded by **Lord Arthur Charles Hervey**, who died in 1894. The present bishop is **Dr G. W. Kennion**, who was translated hither from the Australian diocese of Adelaide.

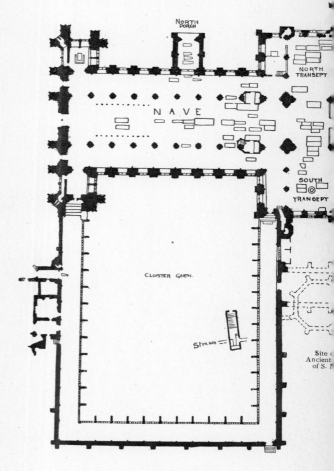

NORTH
PORCH

NORTH
TRANSEPT

NAVE

SOUTH
TRANSEPT

CLOISTER GARTH.

Stream

Site of
Ancient
of S. N

PLAN OF WELLS CATHEDRAL

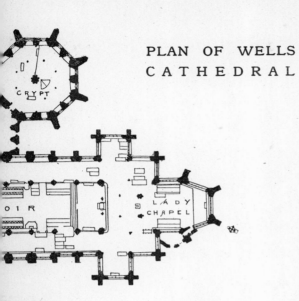

DIMENSIONS OF THE CATHEDRAL

		Feet
Total length	. . . .	385
,, of Nave	. . .	161
,, of Choir	. . .	103
Breadth of Nave	. . .	38
,, ,, with Aisles	. .	82
,, Transepts	. . .	135
Height of Nave	. . .	67
,, Choir	. . .	67
,, Towers	. . .	160
Breadth of West Front	. . .	147

Bell's Cathedral Series.

EDITED BY
GLEESON WHITE AND E. F. STRANGE.

In specially designed cloth cover, crown 8vo, 1s. 6d. each.

Now Ready.

CANTERBURY. By HARTLEY WITHERS. 2nd Edition, revised. 36 Illustrations.
SALISBURY. By GLEESON WHITE. 2nd Edition, revised. 50 Illustrations.
CHESTER. By CHARLES HIATT. 24 Illustrations.
ROCHESTER. By G. H. PALMER, B.A. 38 Illustrations.
OXFORD. By Rev. PERCY DEARMER, M.A. 34 Illustrations.
EXETER. By PERCY ADDLESHAW, B.A. 35 Illustrations.
WINCHESTER. By P. W. SERGEANT. 50 Illustrations.
LICHFIELD. By A. B. CLIFTON. 42 Illustrations.
NORWICH. By C. H. B. QUENNELL. 38 Illustrations.
PETERBOROUGH. By Rev. W. D. SWEETING. 51 Illustrations.
HEREFORD. By A. HUGH FISHER, G.R.E. 34 Illustrations.
LINCOLN. By A. B. KENDRICK, B.A. 46 Illustrations.
WELLS. By Rev. PERCY DEARMER, M.A. 46 Illustrations.
SOUTHWELL. By Rev. ARTHUR DIMOCK, M.A.

In the Press.

DURHAM. By J. E. BYGATE. | GLOUCESTER. By H. L. MASSÉ.
              YORK. By A. CLUTTON BROCK, B.A.

Preparing.

ST. DAVID'S. By PHILIP ROBSON. | CHICHESTER. By H. CORLETTE,
ELY. By T. D. ATKINSON, A.R.I.B.A. | A.R.I.B.A.
WORCESTER. By E. F. STRANGE.
    ST. ALBANS.   RIPON.   ST. PAUL'S.
    CARLISLE.   BRISTOL.

Uniform with above Series.

ST. MARTIN'S, CANTERBURY. By the Rev. CANON ROUTLEDGE.   [*Ready.*
BEVERLEY MINSTER. By CHARLES HIATT.   [*In the Press.*

Opinions of the Press.

"For the purpose at which they aim they are admirably done, and there are few visitants to any of our noble shrines who will not enjoy their visit the better for being furnished with one of these delightful books, which can be slipped into the pocket and carried with ease, and is yet distinct and legible. . . . A volume such as that on Canterbury is exactly what we want, and on our next visit we hope to have it with us. It is thoroughly helpful, and the views of the fair city and its noble cathedral are beautiful. Both volumes, moreover, will serve more than a temporary purpose, and are trustworthy as well as delightful."—*Notes and Queries.*

"We have so frequently in these columns urged the want of cheap, well-illustrated, and well-written handbooks to our cathedrals, to take the place of the out-of-date publications of local booksellers, that we are glad to hear that they have been taken in hand by Messrs George Bell & Sons."—*St. James's Gazette.*

"Visitors to the cathedral cities of England must often have felt the need of some work dealing with the history and antiquities of the city itself, and the architecture and associations of the cathedral, more portable than the elaborate monographs which have been devoted to some of them, more scholarly and satisfying than the average local guide-book, and more copious than the section devoted to them in the general guide-book of the county or district. Such a legitimate need the 'Cathedral Series' now being issued by Messrs George Bell & Sons, under the editorship of Mr Gleeson White and Mr E. F. Strange, seems well calculated to supply. The volumes are handy in size, moderate in price, well illustrated, and written in a scholarly spirit. The history of cathedral and city is intelligently set forth and accompanied by a descriptive survey of the building in all its detail. The illustrations are copious and well selected, and the series bids fair to become an indispensable companion to the cathedral tourist in England."—*Times*.

"They are nicely produced in good type, on good paper, and contain numerous illustrations, are well written, and very cheap. We should imagine architects and students of architecture will be sure to buy the series as they appear, for they contain in brief much valuable information." —*British Architect*.

"Half the charm of this little book on Canterbury springs from the writer's recognition of the historical association of so majestic a building with the fortunes, destinies, and habits of the English people. . . . One admirable feature of the book is its artistic illustrations. They are both lavish and satisfactory—even when regarded with critical eyes."— *Speaker*.

"There is likely to be a large demand for these attractive handbooks." —*Globe*.

"Bell's 'Cathedral Series,' so admirably edited, is more than a description of the various English cathedrals. It will be a valuable historical record, and a work of much service also to the architect. The illustrations are well selected, and in many cases not mere bald architectural drawings but reproductions of exquisite stone fancies, touched in their treatment by fancy and guided by art."—*Star*.

"Each of them contains exactly that amount of information which the intelligent visitor, who is not a specialist, will wish to have. The disposition of the various parts is judiciously proportioned, and the style is very readable. The illustrations supply a further important feature ; they are both numerous and good. A series which cannot fail to be welcomed by all who are interested in the ecclesiastical buildings of England."— *Glasgow Herald*.

"Those who, either for purposes of professional study or for a cultured recreation, find it expedient to 'do' the English cathedrals will welcome the beginning of Bell's 'Cathedral Series.' This set of books is an attempt to consult, more closely, and in greater detail than the usual guide-books do, the needs of visitors to the cathedral towns. The series cannot but prove markedly successful. In each book a business-like description is given of the fabric of the church to which the volume relates, and an interesting history of the relative diocese. The books are plentifully illustrated, and are thus made attractive as well as instructive. They cannot but prove welcome to all classes of readers interested either in English Church history or in ecclesiastical architecture."—*Scotsman*.

"A set of little books which may be described as very useful, very pretty, and very cheap . . . . and alike in the letterpress, the illustrations, and the remarkably choice binding, they are ideal guides."— *Liverpool Daily Post*.

"They have nothing in common with the almost invariably wretched local guides save portability, and their only competitors in the quality and quantity of their contents are very expensive and mostly rare works, each of a size that suggests a packing-case rather than a coat-pocket. The 'Cathedral Series' are important compilations concerning history, architecture, and biography, and quite popular enough for such as take any sincere interest in their subjects."—*Sketch*.

LONDON: GEORGE BELL AND SONS.